The Army of the Early Roman Empire 30 BC–AD 180

The Army of the Early Roman Empire 30 BC–AD 180

History, Organization and Equipment

Gabriele Esposito

Pen & Sword
MILITARY

First published in Great Britain in 2022
by Pen & Sword Military
An imprint of Pen & Sword Books Limited
47 Church Street
Barnsley
South Yorkshire
S70 2AS

ISBN 978 1 52678 739 2

A CIP catalogue record for this book is
available from the British Library

Typeset in Adobe Caslon
by Mac Style

Printed and bound in India by Replika Press Pvt. Ltd.

Pen & Sword Books Limited incorporates the imprints of Atlas,
Archaeology, Aviation, Discovery, Family History, Fiction, History, Maritime,
Military, Military Classics, Politics, Select, Transport, True Crime, Air World,
Frontline Publishing, Leo Cooper, Remember When, Seaforth Publishing,
The Praetorian Press, Wharncliffe Local History, Wharncliffe Transport,
Wharncliffe True Crime and White Owl.

For a complete list of Pen & Sword titles please contact
PEN & SWORD BOOKS LIMITED
47 Church Street, Barnsley, South Yorkshire, S70 2AS, England
E mail: enquiries@pen-and-sword.co.uk
Website: www. pen-and-sword.co.uk

Contents

Gabriele Esposito is a military historian who works as a freelance author and researcher for some of the most important publishing houses in the military history sector. In particular, he is an expert specializing in uniformology: his interests and expertise range from the ancient civilizations to modern post-colonial conflicts. During recent years, he has conducted and published several researches on the military history of the Latin American countries, with special attention on the War of the Triple Alliance and the War of the Pacific. He is among the leading experts on the military history of the Italian Wars of Unification and the Spanish Carlist Wars. His books and essays are published on a regular basis by Osprey Publishing, Winged Hussar Publishing and Libreria Editrice Goriziana; he is also the author of numerous military history articles appearing in specialized magazines like *Ancient Warfare Magazine*, *Medieval Warfare Magazine*, *The Armourer*, *History of War*, *Guerres et Histoire*, *Focus Storia* and *Focus Storia Wars*.

Acknowledgements

This book is dedicated to my magnificent parents, Maria Rosaria and Benedetto, for the immense love and fundamental support that they always give me. Their precious advice over many years has helped to make the present book a much better one than it otherwise would have been. A very special thanks goes to Philip Sidnell, the commissioning editor of my books for Pen & Sword: his love for history and his passion for publishing are the key factors behind the success of our publications. Many thanks also to the production manager of this title, Matt Jones, for his excellent work and great enthusiasm. A special thanks is due to Tony Walton for editing my original manuscript in a highly professional way. A very special mention goes to the brilliant re-enactment groups that collaborated, with their photographs, on the creation of this book: without the incredible work of research of their members, the final result of this publication would have not been the same. As a result, I want to express my deep gratitude to the following living history associations: Ala I Batavorum from the Netherlands (especially Jurjen Draaisma), Legio II Traiana Fortis – Cohors I Barcinonum, Barcino Oriens from Catalonia (especially Marc Seriol), Legio XI C.P.F. Hispaniensis from Spain (especially Iago Rodriguez Diaz), Legio XIIII Gemina from the USA (especially David Burns) and Lorica Romana from France (especially Marilyn Paléri).

Introduction

The main aim of this book is to present a detailed overview of the Roman Army's history, organization and equipment during the early centuries of the Empire. Our analysis will start from the year 30 BC, which saw the ascendancy of Octavianus Augustus as the princeps (first one, or leader) of Rome. Augustus, the first Emperor of Rome, was able to restore peace and order in the Roman territories after six decades of civil wars that had almost destroyed the political power of Rome. When he became the sole ruler of Rome, Augustus faced a very difficult situation: the economy had been shattered by the terrible military events of recent years, society was divided into opposing groups with contrasting interests and the military consisted of too many professional soldiers who now risked becoming unemployed. The political power of Rome had been seriously damaged by the civil wars: several peripheral territories were in revolt, some areas still had to be pacified and the system of client kings had to be restructured. The traditional Roman virtues of valour and honour, which had guided the senators and the generals of the Roman Republic during previous centuries, seemed to be lost: Rome needed a restoration, but also needed to adopt a new form of government. The civil wars had clearly shown that Rome's territories were too extensive to be governed by an assembly like the Senate, which was made up of politicians who had contrasting political interests. The institutions of the Republic had worked well when Rome controlled just the Italian peninsula, but now that the whole Mediterranean was under Roman control, a more effective and centralized form of government was desperately needed. Each of the territories that made up the late Roman Republic had a different institutional status: some were provinces, others were client states ruled by vassal kings, and there were also allied states with a higher degree of autonomy. This organizational chaos had to be changed in order for Roman-held territories to have more cohesion.

During the last civil war of the Republic, Octavianus Augustus had defeated Mark Antony and had added Egypt to Roman territories. Egypt was not ruled as a normal province, but as a special one placed under the direct control of the princeps. As a result, the occupation of Egypt augmented the institutional fragmentation that characterized Roman territories during the late years of the Republic. To solve all Rome's problems, Augustus decided to transform the Roman Republic into an empire ruled by a single man. However, he knew that such a major political change would not readily be accepted by the Senate and the Roman oligarchies. Just fifteen years previously, his mentor, Julius Caesar, had tried to do something similar, but had paid for it with his life when he was assassinated in the Senate by members of the Roman aristocracy. As a result, Augustus had to move very cautiously to carry out his planned reform without causing strong opposition among the Senate. Having the loyal support of the common citizens, who were tired of civil wars and wanted only peace, he gradually took all the most important powers from the Senate but without abolishing any of the aristocrats' privileges. The Senate continued to function, the republican institutions were preserved and – at least on paper – Rome's form of government was not changed. Augustus thus assumed the title of princeps, which is different from that of emperor; he did not have absolute powers like the emperors who followed him, and always respected the prerogatives of the Senate. Augustus defined himself as a *primum inter pares*, a 'first among peers', in order to show his personal respect for the aristocracy. The Senate, understanding that a collaboration with the princeps could have only positive consequences, accepted Augustus' reforms with a degree of enthusiasm, and did not oppose Rome's transition from Republic to Empire. This change was completed within a few years without any significant problem. Over time, Augustus became increasingly popular and started to transform the new form of government – known as the principate – into a form of hereditary monarchy. When he died, in AD 14, the Senate had already become a purely ornamental institution, since all the powers were now in the hands of the emperor: the transition had been smooth but effective, and the Roman Empire had effectively been born. Until AD 180, the successors of Augustus ruled Rome as absolute monarchs, expanding their territories by launching several victorious military campaigns in what is commonly known as the early Empire.

Chapter 1

The Roman Army of the Principate

From the beginning of his rule as princeps, Augustus presented himself as a sincere defender of peace: he recognized that Roman society needed a new period of peace and prosperity after having been shattered by terrible internal divisions. Internal order was restored by cleaning up the countryside of the bands of brigands that had been ravaging it, as well as by dissolving all the political associations that were still related to the defunct leaders of the civil wars. Augustus paid particular attention to improving the living conditions of the poorest social groups. He reduced the number of slaves and divided them into a series of new categories, each of which had some duties but also some rights. Furthermore, he cancelled all the debts that had been contracted by the poorest citizens during the civil wars and reorganized local administration by introducing middle-class men (the equites) into them. He also promoted demographic expansion with the promulgation of some specific laws, regulated the monetary market in order to initiate a period of economic growth and distributed the lands confiscated during the civil conflicts to his veteran soldiers or to farmers of proven loyalty. Augustus restored the traditional religion and morality of Rome, after decades of bloody crimes, ordered the construction of many important public infrastructures, most notably of roads and aqueducts, and launched an ambitious cultural programme which supported his political propaganda and was based on the importance of literature (it was under Augustus, for example, that Virgil wrote the epic poem *The Aeneid*). All these measures had a deep impact over the life of the ordinary citizens and soon gave both Roman society and the economy a period of great renaissance.

In addition to improving the living conditions of the citizens inside the Empire, however, Augustus also had to deal with the defence of the long borders of his domains. The first thing that had to be done was a general reorganization of the various Roman territories from an institutional and administrative point of view. In 27 BC, all the regions of the Empire – except for the Italian peninsula, which had a special status – were reorganized as provinces. These could be of two different kinds: *provinciae pacate* and *provinciae non pacate*. The former consisted of those territories that had been conquered for many years by the Romans and were thus considered fully pacified since they were not exposed to serious military threats. The

Roman legionary of the early Principate with *lorica hamata*. The *pilum* is of a lesser-known model, still popular during Augustus' reign. (*Photo and copyright by Marilyn Paléri of the historical reconstitution association Lorica Romana*)

Roman legionary of the early Principate with *lorica hamata*. The decorative eyes painted on the helmet had an apotropaic function. (*Photo and copyright by Marilyn Paléri of the historical reconstitution association Lorica Romana*)

provinciae non pacate, meanwhile, were those territories in which some form of local opposition to the Roman presence still existed or that were particularly exposed to foreign attacks. The *provinciae pacate* were placed under the direct jurisdiction of Augustus, together with the large military contingents that garrisoned them, whereas the *provinciae non pacate* continued to be governed by governors (*proconsules*), who were aristocrats chosen by the Senate. The provinces controlled by the emperor were governed by officials known as *legati Augusti pro praetore*, who were extremely loyal to Augustus and usually had solid military skills. The taxes collected in the *provinciae pacate* became part of the *aerarium*, the treasury of the Roman state controlled by the Senate, while those raised in the *provinciae non pacate* became part of the *fiscus*, the new treasury of the princeps that was created by Augustus. The provinces under control of the Senate were very few, but quite rich, comprising southern Spain, the coastline of Tunisia and Algeria, the western half of Anatolia, Greece, Macedonia and southern France. All the rest of the Roman Empire was under the direct rule of the emperor. Augustus progressively reduced the number of client kingdoms that were located on the borders of Roman territory by absorbing them into the Empire. In addition, he ordered the foundation of many new Roman colonies in the various provinces, with the objective of augmenting the number of Italic people who lived in the peripheral areas of the Empire. The princeps formed a very strong alliance with the middle-class of the equites, who became the backbone of his new Imperial administration. These men now had the possibility to create a brilliant career in the provinces thanks to their technical skills and their loyalty to the emperor, which had been impossible while the Senate continued to exert a strict control over the administration of the Roman Republic. Power and wealth were now distributed in a more egalitarian way, something that greatly increased the emperor's popularity.

When Augustus became princeps, the Roman Army was already a deadly military machine that was made up of professional soldiers. Following the Battle of Arausio in 105 BC, when a large Roman army was annihilated by Germanic tribesmen, Rome's military forces had been completely reformed by Gaius Marius, the great general and consul. Marius decided to transform the Roman Army into a force made up of professional fighters coming from the poorest social groups of the Republic. These would serve in the army for most of their life and were equipped by the state. The era of the republican citizen/soldier was over: the new professional soldiers earned a living thanks to their military career and were available to serve in every corner of the Mediterranean world, with no time limits. Gaius Marius greatly improved the training and discipline of the Roman armies, giving to each soldier a heavy personal equipment that included various working tools, allowing each legionary (heavy infantryman) to operate as a combat engineer if needed, able to build fortified encampments or to destroy the fortifications of the enemy. The ambitious general and consul strove to create a new *esprit de corps* inside the legions: he was the first, for example, to give a distinctive standard and a peculiar denomination to each unit of the Roman Army. With the outbreak of the civil wars, the military reforms carried out by Marius were tested to the limit. The opposing factions recruited armies with many thousands of professional legionaries, which destroyed each other in some of the bloodiest battles ever fought in Antiquity. From a qualitative point of view, no army of the Mediterranean world could face the new Roman legions on equal terms: they were better disciplined, trained, equipped and commanded than any of their potential opponents.

When the civil wars came to an end in 30 BC, however, it became clear that the immense military machine that had been mobilized during the previous decades had to be greatly reduced in number. The finances of Rome could no longer sustain the costs of keeping in service an army with sixty legions and 300,000 men. It should be noted that during the last years of the civil wars, several new legions had been formed with soldiers of inferior quality. On occasions, every able-bodied man of a territory had been forced to enlist as a legionary, while the armies of several client kings had been transformed into legions. As a result, to create some form of peace establishment, Augustus had to drastically reduce the number of legions, which he did by choosing the best legionaries who would remain in the service of Rome. The new Roman Army consisted of volunteers who wished to serve the Empire as professional soldiers for two decades of their lives. They were loyal to the emperor more than to any other Roman institution. In order to be sure of his soldiers' loyalty, Augustus created the *aerarium militare*, or military treasure, which was specifically tasked with paying the legionaries with both precision and regularity. The emperor knew full well that the only way to avoid mutinies and rebellions was to pay the soldiers well (he increased their standard pay) and to offer them acceptable living conditions. Once a legionary completed his period of service, he was given a farm by the state in compensation for his twenty years of service to Rome. As a result of these improved terms and conditions, the legions of the Roman Army began to consist of determined and disciplined men who believed that loyalty towards the emperor could guarantee them success in their personal life. To find the economic resources needed to create the *aerarium militare*, Augustus had no choice but to cut costs. Consequently, after 30 BC, the total number of legions was rapidly reduced from sixty to just twenty-eight, with only the best elements of the Roman Army being retained in service. In order to avoid the outbreak of revolts, Augustus gave donatives and lands to most of the veterans who were discharged from the Army (even to the many who had served in Mark Antony's legions). During the period of the civil wars, the survival

Roman veteran legionary of the early Principate, drinking from his canteen covered with wicker. The Celtic torque neck rings, worn as decorations, have probably been taken from dead enemies. (Photo and copyright by Legio XIIII Gemina)

of a Roman soldier depended on the decisions of his commander, from whom he received his pay as well as land and property at the end of his career. Augustus, after his ascendancy to power, changed all this, cancelling the private dimension that had been acquired by the Roman military forces. The legionaries remained professional soldiers, but started to be paid by the central administration of the state. The farms given to the veterans were now also to be provided by the imperial administration, and thus the loyalty of the soldiers started to shift from their commanders to the ruling imperial dynasty.

The main military unit of Augustus' Roman Army was the legion: a large heavy infantry formation, entirely composed of volunteers with Roman citizenship. Each

Roman legionary of the early Principate, with *lorica hamata*. The bronze disks and red leather straps were worn as military decorations only by the veteran soldiers. (*Photo and copyright by Legio XI C.P.F. Hispaniensis*)

legion comprised some 5,500 men, divided into one elite *Cohors Prima* and nine 'line' cohorts. The First Cohort, formed by the best soldiers of the legion, had 800 men, whereas the other nine cohorts numbered 480 legionaries each. The *Cohors Prima* had five centuries of 160 men each, while the normal cohorts had six centuries of eighty legionaries each. Each *centuria* was made up of ten smaller units, formed by seven soldiers plus a single NCO known as a *decanus* and two non-combatants. This *contubernium* was the smallest unit existing in the Roman Army. In addition, each legion had its own cavalry component: 120 cavalrymen divided into four *turmae*, with thirty soldiers in each. The *turma* was structured on three *decuriae*, the smallest cavalry units, each of which comprised eight soldiers, a *Decurio* (the equivalent of the infantry centurion) and an *Optio* (acting as an NCO). Most of the legionaries came from Italy, but as time progressed the provincial elements became increasingly numerous. The system of ranks of the Roman legion was quite complex, being specifically designed to make such a large body of soldiers work properly.

The overall commander of the legion was the *Legatus Legionis*, usually a senator appointed by the emperor. As time progressed, however, many members of the *equites* social class became commanders of a legion. If a legion was garrisoned in a province where no other legions were located, its commander also acted as provincial governor; when performing these functions, he was commonly known as the *Legatus Augusti pro praetore*. The second officer in the chain of command was the *Tribunus Laticlavius*, who was generally a young member of the Senate with no military experience, having been assigned to the command of a legion in order to learn from the legate. The third in command was the *Praefectus Castrorum*, who was responsible for the building and defence of the legion's camp. He was a long-serving veteran from the *equites*, who had already completed his twenty years of service and had served as the most senior centurion in a legion. His functions included the training of soldiers and of new recruits. The group of senior officers was completed by five lower-ranking tribunes known as *Tribuni Augusticlavii*, who were all from the equestrian class and already had a certain level of military experience. They mainly performed administrative functions and commanded two cohorts each.

The most senior centurion in a legion, called the *Primus Pilus*, commanded the first century of the elite First Cohort. Once in battle, he had the honour to command the entire *Cohors Prima*. The other five centurions of the First Cohort were known as *Primi Ordines* and were considered to be superior in rank to their equivalents in the other cohorts. The centurions commanding the first centuries of the nine regular cohorts were called the *Pili Priores* and were superior in rank to the *Primi Ordines* of the First Cohort. Like the *Primus Pilus*, each of these officers took command of his entire cohort in the event of a battle. Generally speaking, all centurions came from the lower social classes and became officers only thanks to their personal capabilities, making these experienced veterans the true backbone of the Roman Army. The commander of the four cavalry *turmae* was known as the *Tribunus Sexmentris*; the decurion commanding each first *decuria* of horsemen had the honour to lead the entire *turma* in battle. The rank organization of the NCOs was particularly articulated, in order to perform a wide range of different functions. Each centurion directly appointed his adjutant and second in command, the *Optio*, who performed more or less the same commanding functions as the centurion, but during battle he had the important responsibility of remaining at the back of the century in order to keep the formation closed and to discourage deserters from abandoning the field. Each *Optio* had an adjutant known as a *Tesserarius*, who was third in the century's chain of command. The *Tesserarius* was the keeper of the watchword of his unit and performed several important administrative functions. The system of NCOs was completed by the ten *Decani*, each of whom commanded one of the *contubernia* that made up a century. Two auxiliary servants were assigned to each *contubernium*.

Common legionaries could perform a series of special duties, each of which had a specific designation and corresponded to higher pay. The most important of these was that of *Aquilifer*. The *Aquila* was the legion's standard and represented the valour of the whole unit; losing it was the greatest dishonour that a Roman legion could endure. As a result of this symbolic importance, its bearer was chosen from among the most experienced veteran soldiers. Each cohort had its own *Vexillum* (standard) that was carried by a special bearer known as the *Vexillifer*, while each century had its own *Signum* that was carried by a *Signifer*. The *Signum* consisted of a spear shaft decorated with medallions and topped with an open hand to signify loyalty towards the state. In addition to the above, the *Cohors Prima* had the privilege to carry a special image of the emperor, which was given to an elite bearer known as the *Imaginifer*. Finally, each century had its own military music, consisting of a *Cornicen* or *Bucinator* and a *Tubicen*. These musicians transmitted orders by playing their instruments and usually acted in close combination with the *Signifer*, who was a rallying point for all the legionaries. The *Cornicen* played a horn, the *Bucinator* had a particular kind of horn known as a *buccina*, and the *Tubicen* played a long trumpet. Each legion deployed its own artillery: individual cohorts had a stone-throwing *ballista* and each century was responsible for a bolt-shooting *scorpio*. A single Roman legion could thus deploy an impressive artillery detachment, with ten heavy *ballistae* and fifty-nine light *scorpiones*.

Under the military reforms carried out by Gaius Marius during the Cimbrian War, the Roman legions adopted a new structure that did not comprise light infantry but only *cohortes* of heavy infantry. As a result of this, the Romans had to

Roman legionary with lorica segmentata and rectangular shield. (*Photo by Marc Seriol [@marcmarkhus_photo] and copyright by Legio II Traiana Fortis – Cohors I Barcinonum, Barcino Oriens*)

Roman legionary with the woollen cloak that was worn during cold months. (*Photo and copyright by Legio XIIII Gemina*)

rely on foreign soldiers during the late Republican period in order to deploy sizeable contingents of light troops. The same happened with the cavalry, which had never been a fundamental component of the Roman Army. During his Gallic campaigns, for example, Julius Caesar deployed the following auxiliary contingents: Celtic heavy cavalrymen, Germanic light cavalrymen, African mounted skirmishers recruited from the Numidians and the Mauri, Cretan archers, Balearic slingers and Iberian light infantrymen. The Celtic heavy cavalry came from the tribes of Gaul that were allied with Rome, most notably from the Aedui. They were equipped with helmet and chainmail, and were armed with spears and long slashing swords. Mounted on tall horses, these cavalrymen made up a shock force that was employed with great success by Caesar on several occasions. The Germanic light cavalrymen were equipped as light skirmishers, having no armour or helmets and being armed with throwing javelins. These horsemen were of great use for conducting reconnaissance missions as well as harassing the enemy with rapid incursions. On some occasions they were also employed to launch frontal charges, and they were generally considered by Caesar to be a fundamental component of his military forces. In 55 BC, the Roman troops operating in Gaul included a total of 400 Germani, who were all nobles from the tribes that had been defeated by Caesar and who served alongside the Romans (together with their servants) as hostages. Their presence on Rome's side was a sign of goodwill and trust, which had great political importance. Julius Caesar was particularly impressed by the martial spirit of the Germani, admiring them for their courage and their simple way of life (which was ideal to forge good warriors). The 400 Germanic cavalrymen who served as part of Caesar's army were supported by a number of light infantrymen, the servants of the Germanic nobles who were trained to run with the horsemen in order to cover their flanks during close combat. Caesar encountered this peculiar tactical formation invented by the Germani during the campaign fought against their leader Ariovistus, and soon understood that it had great potential. Consequently, he was the first to create combined units of infantry and cavalry inside the Roman Army, who became known as *cohortes equitate* and remained an important component of the Roman military for a long time.

With the outbreak of Vercingetorix's rebellion in Gaul, many allied Celtic horsemen abandoned Caesar, who was obliged to recruit more Germani in order to replace them. There were 600 of these in total, as usual accompanied by their servants as light infantrymen. The Germanic warriors of Caesar fought with great valour on several occasions against the forces of Vercingetorix, always routing the Celtic cavalry that opposed them. The Germani who participated in the final Gallic campaign of 52 BC also followed Caesar during the ensuing years, taking part in all the conflicts that were fought by their general, most notably in the civil war that ended with the defeat of Pompey at the Battle of Pharsalus in 48 BC. In 45 BC, Caesar returned to Rome and disbanded the auxiliary corps of his army, the surviving Germanic veterans going back to their homeland after having travelled around the Mediterranean and plundered many different countries.

The Numidians and the Mauri serving with Caesar were equipped as mounted skirmishers and used javelins as their main weapon. Like they had previously done as part of Hannibal's Carthaginian army, they performed as explorers and were recognized as masters at organizing ambushes. Cretan archers and Balearic slingers were mercenaries who were well known in the Mediterranean world for their incredible fighting skills. Crete and the Balearic Islands were the home of two of the most important 'light infantry schools' of Antiquity, where the deadliest archers and slingers were trained as professional soldiers from their childhood. The Iberian light infantrymen were known as *caetrati*, from the small round shield they carried called the *caetra*. They were armed with deadly short swords and javelins, and Caesar appreciated them for their great tactical flexibility.

When Augustus reformed the structure of the Roman Army, he decided that the foreign contingents of light infantry and cavalry described above should become a fixed component of Rome's military forces. Until that moment, these light and mounted contingents had been recruited on a temporary basis and had always been disbanded at the end of the various military campaigns. They did not have a standardized organization and could be commanded by their own officers, who were mercenaries paid by the Roman Republic. Augustus changed all this by transforming the provisional corps of light infantry and cavalry into a permanent component of his new Roman Army: the *auxilia*, or auxiliaries. These were commanded by Roman officers and received regular pay from the imperial government, as a result of which they lost their previous mercenary status and became a regular military institution. The new auxiliaries, like their predecessors, were recruited on a local basis from the provincial inhabitants of the Empire, and thus provided contingents with different tactical features, coming from every corner of the Roman world. Differently from the legionaries, they were not Roman citizens, but after twenty-five years of honoured military service they were granted Roman citizenship and a farm located in their home province. Thanks to the new system introduced by Augustus, serving in the *auxilia* units became the best way for a provincial to become a Roman citizen and to improve his social position. Thanks to the sacrifices of his father, the son of a provincial auxiliary could enlist in the Roman Army as a legionary. A new hereditary class of provincial soldiers was soon formed, with men who were strongly linked to their home provinces but at the same time were extremely loyal to Rome thanks to the opportunity of social improvement that they had received.

Roman legionary with *lorica segmentata*. (*Photo and copyright by Legio XI C.P.F. Hispaniensis*)

Roman legionary with *lorica segmentata* and leather pteruges. (*Photo and copyright by Legio XI C.P.F. Hispaniensis*)

As time progressed, the auxiliary units increased their level of professionalism and started to be sent campaigning across the Empire, meaning the central government in Rome could avoid the outbreak of revolts of auxiliary units supported by the population of their own provinces. With the expansion and consolidation of the Empire, new military traditions were gradually absorbed into the Roman Army thanks to the *auxilia* system, such as archers recruited from the eastern provinces or camel troops. The Romans first encountered camel-mounted troops when they fought against the Seleucid Antiochus III in 190 BC, but it was only during the second century AD that a Roman camel corps was formed. In AD 106, the emperor Trajan added to the Empire the new province of Arabia Petraea and thus created the Ala I Ulpia Dromedariorum Palmyrenorum, which was formed with camel warriors from the city of Palmyra. In the following decades, the Romans formed various small *auxilia* units of *dromedarii*, which proved to be very effective in patrolling the desert frontiers of the Empire. Their tasks included escorting convoys, defending important routes of communication, scouting in the desert, escorting couriers and battling against desert bandits. They were organized in small squads, having special bases in the desert that provided them with food and water.

Basically, there were three different kinds of *auxilia* units: *cohortes* of all infantry, *alae* of all cavalry and *cohortes equitate* (infantry cohorts with an attached cavalry contingent). The cohorts had the same internal organization and structure as the legionary ones, albeit acting as light infantry units. The *alae* were the proper cavalry of the Roman Army, since the few cavalrymen of the legions performed only auxiliary duties to the functions of the heavy infantry (for example escorting officers, transmitting orders or scouting). The *alae* could be either of heavy or light cavalry, but were all characterized by the quality of their specific training. The *cohortes equitate* – created by Julius Caesar – were a mix of foot and mounted auxiliaries, a smaller replica of the larger legions: thanks to the presence of some horsemen, they could act as autonomous small armies for service on the frontier. Each of these three kinds of unit could have two different establishments, with either 500 or 1,000 men. A *cohors quingenaria* had six centuries of eighty soldiers, with a *Praefectus* as commander; a *cohors miliaria* had ten centuries of eighty soldiers, commanded by a *Tribunus Militum*. The *ala quingenaria* had sixteen *turmae* of thirty men, with a *Praefectus* as commander; the *ala miliaria* had twenty-four *turmae* of thirty men and always commanded by a *Praefectus*. A *cohors equitata quingenaria* had six centuries of eighty infantry and four *turmae* of thirty cavalry, commanded by a *Praefectus*; a *cohors equitata miliaria* had ten centuries of eighty infantrymen and eight *turmae* of thirty cavalrymen, with a *Tribunus Milituum* in command.

During military campaigns, the various auxiliary units were attached to the legions, thus coming under the direct control of the legionary commanders. Most of the *auxilia* units were stationed on the vast borders of the Empire, together with the legions. The frontiers were the only points from which enemy attacks could come, and so this defensive disposition of the Roman forces was quite logical. It should be pointed out, however, that in the event of internal disturbances, very few fighting men were available to face threats coming from the inside of the Empire. There was no central military reserve, and it was practically impossible to take a full legion from its frontier garrison without creating a major gap in the border defences. The only possible solution to this serious problem was to take detachments from various legions and assemble them together in order to form temporary task forces known as *vexillationes*. As soon as the internal emergency was resolved, a temporary *vexillatio* was dissolved and its detachments were sent back to their parent legions. Usually, a *vexillatio* was a mixed force of legionaries and auxiliaries, composed of 1,000 infantry and 500 horsemen: two infantry cohorts taken from a legion and a single *ala quingenaria* of mounted auxiliaries.

The military situation in Italy and the city of Rome was quite different from that in the provinces. The capital was the heart of the Empire, where the emperor and the entire central administration worked. Under the reforms of Sulla and according to an ancient Roman tradition, no military units could enter the Italian peninsula without being seen as a menace by the institutions of Rome: the territory of Italy was thus considered sacred by the Romans, who called it the *pomerium*. This area corresponded more or less to modern Italy: the River Rubicon in the north and the Straits of Messina in the south were its natural borders. Consequently, Italy could not be garrisoned by legions or auxiliary units like all the other provinces. Yet the emperor and the city of Rome obviously needed some military forces for their protection, especially against any internal threats. Augustus resolved this issue by creating the Praetorian Guard. This elite unit, formally the personal guard of the emperors, also acted as the garrison of the Italian peninsula. Initially, it was formed from the best soldiers serving with the legions, so it represented the cream of the Roman Army. Created by Augustus and later reorganized by his successor, Tiberius, the Praetorian Guard was structured on nine infantry cohorts. Under the first emperor, three cohorts were stationed in Rome and the other six in other important cities around Italy. However, during the reign of Tiberius, all the Praetorians were garrisoned in Rome, in the famous barracks known as the *Castra Praetoria*. The whole Praetorian Guard was commanded by a *Praefectus Praetorio*, who came from the ranks of the *equites*. Each cohort was commanded by a *Tribunus Militum* and had six centuries of eighty soldiers. The original number of nine cohorts was later changed on several occasions: around AD 47, they were increased to twelve, and they became sixteen in AD 69 (under Vitellius, who also augmented their internal establishment from 500 to 1,000 men

Roman veteran legionary with *lorica segmentata* and *vexillum*. (*Photo and copyright by Legio XIIII Gemina*)

Roman legionary with *lorica segmentata*. (*Photo and copyright by Marilyn Paléri of the historical reconstitution association Lorica Romana*)

each). Vespasian reduced the number of cohorts again to nine (with 500 men each), while Domitian increased it to ten, setting the definitive establishment that would not change until the final dissolution of the corps. Initially, all the Praetorians were ex-legionaries who hailed from Italy, but over time the presence of provincials became increasingly important. The soldiers of the Praetorian Guard had many privileges compared with the regular legionaries: their period of service lasted for sixteen years instead of twenty, and their pay was significantly higher than that of normal soldiers. Trajan added a cavalry component to the Praetorian Guard, the members of which were known as *Equites singulares Augusti*. These mounted Praetorians escorted the emperor whenever he left Rome for a military campaign or for a journey around the provinces. The *Equites singulares Augusti* were organized like a normal *ala miliaria*, with twenty-four turmae of thirty men and a *Tribunus Militum* at their head. All the members of this unit were selected from the best horsemen of the auxiliary *alae*, and were granted Roman citizenship upon enlisting into the Praetorian Guard.

The military reforms of Augustus that affected the garrison of Italy were not limited to the creation of the Praetorian Guard, as he also formed another two corps that were to be stationed in Rome: the *Urbaniciani* and the *Vigiles*. The *Urbaniciani* were a sort of police force, whose main function was to keep order in the immense city of Rome. If the Praetorians were the protectors of the emperor, the *Urbaniciani* were the protectors of Rome. While the Praetorian Guard was under the direct control of the emperor, the *Urbaniciani* were the only Roman military unit still under the control of the Senate: their commander, the *Praefectus Urbi*, was in fact a senator. Initially, the *Urbaniciani* consisted of three cohorts, numbered progressively after the nine of the Praetorians, with each single cohort commanded by a *Tribunus Militum* and having six centuries of eighty soldiers. The original three cohorts were later expanded to seven during the reign of Claudius, while Vitellius increased the size of each cohort to 1,000 men. Unlike the Praetorians, the *Urbaniciani* continued to be recruited from Italy during their entire existence. The other corps created by Augustus and stationed in Rome was the *Vigiles*, who acted as urban guards or firemen. Their main functions amounted to patrolling the capital's streets during the night and fighting fires (which could be destructive for a city at this time, as the 'Great Fire of Rome' clearly showed in AD 64). Their commander was known as the *Praefectus Vigilum* and came from the class of the *equites*, and they were organized in seven *cohortes miliariae* for a total of 7,000 men. Most of their members were *liberti*, i.e. freed slaves of low social condition. Each cohort of the *Vigiles* was commanded by a *Tribunus Militum* and was peculiarly divided into just seven centuries. At the time of Augustus, the city of Rome was divided into fourteen regions, so each cohort of firemen was responsible for the security of two *regiones*. Finally, Augustus created a small corps of foreign bodyguards in order to protect his own person: the *Germani corporis custodes*. This unit was the emperor's private guard, totally independent from the Praetorians, and was entirely composed of Germanic warriors from the Batavian tribe, who acted as personal protectors of the emperor and his family. Being foreigners, they were totally loyal to the monarch and had no links with the internal political situation of Rome. In AD 9, as a result of the catastrophic Roman defeat against the Germanic tribes under Arminius at the Battle of the Teutoburg Forest, this unit was temporarily disbanded. Reformed several years later, the *Germani corporis custodes* were definitively disbanded by Galba in AD 69 because of their strong loyalty to Nero. Initially, these Germanic guards numbered more or less 100, but by the time of Nero they were 500-strong. They were organized in *decuriae*, each of which was led by a decurion.

Roman legionary with *lorica segmentata* and leather pteruges. (*Photo and copyright by Legio XI C.P.F. Hispaniensis*)

Roman centurion (left) and legionary (right), both wearing *lorica segmentata*. (*Photo and copyright by Legio XIIII Gemina*)

Chapter 2

The Military Campaigns of Augustus

Soon after becoming emperor, Augustus had to deal with problems related to the frontiers of Roman territory in 29 BC. Following their victories over Carthage during the Second Punic War, the Romans had occupied a large portion of the Iberian peninsula and had established new provinces in the western Mediterranean world. The resistance of the local Iberian tribes to Roman penetration, however, was particularly strong from the beginning. The Iberians were skilled warriors, who had been the backbone of Hannibal's victorious army. During the period from 200–100 BC, Rome consolidated its position in Iberia by expanding its territorial possessions and crushing several revolts of the local peoples. At the end of this long process, which saw several defeats of the Roman legionaries on the harsh terrain of present-day Spain, most of Iberia had been conquered by the Republic. Only the north-western corner of the Iberian peninsula, consisting of Cantabria and Asturias, remained independent; this area was populated by the Celtiberians, an ethnic group of ancient Spain that was the result of the union between the Celts and Iberians. Cantabria and Asturias, being mostly covered with mountains, had a harsh climate and were quite isolated from the rest of Spain. The outbreak of the civil wars prevented the Romans from completing their conquest of Iberia, since the legions spent most of their time fighting against each other. The Spanish territories of Rome were involved in various conflicts on several occasions, for example when the Roman general Sertorius revolted against the Republic and allied himself with the Iberians (80–72 BC) or when Pompey's legions in Spain were defeated by forces led by Caesar at the Battle of Munda (45 BC). After the end of the civil wars, Augustus decided to complete the pacification of Iberia by conquering Cantabria and Asturias. However, the Celtiberians living in these regions – between the mountains of the Pyrenees and the waters of the Atlantic Ocean, in the wildest part of Spain – were determined to preserve their independence. The Cantabrians had served as mercenaries for both the Carthaginians and the Romans during previous centuries and had been appreciated as light infantrymen by Julius Caesar. The Astures, meanwhile, had always lived in a state of almost complete isolation. Both tribes used guerrilla tactics based on hit-and-run attacks and were expert in mountain warfare. They had a better knowledge of their home territory than the Romans and were absolute masters at organizing ambushes. The standard panoply of the Celtiberian warriors consisted of only light weapons: short swords, daggers, short spears, throwing javelins, small round or oval shields (this type of shield was called the *caetra* by the Romans). Realizing that the conquest of Cantabria and Asturias would be a long and difficult process, the emperor deployed substantial numbers of men against the Celtiberians. The following Roman military formations took part in the various campaigns that were fought by Augustus in northern Iberia:

- I Legio *Augusta*
- II Legio *Augusta*
- IV Legio *Macedonica*
- V Legio *Alaudae*
- VI Legio *Victrix*
- IX Legio *Hispana*
- X Legio *Gemina*
- XX Legio *Valeria Victrix*
- Ala *Augusta*
- Ala *Parthorum*
- Ala *II Gallorum*
- Ala *II Thracum Victrix Civium Romanorum*
- Cohors *II Gallorum*
- Cohors *IV Thracum Aequitata*

The first years of the conflict, from 29–26 BC, saw little progress for the Romans, who were unable to penetrate into enemy territory. The elusive tactics of the Celtiberians prevented them from obtaining a decisive victory in the open field. During the latter months of 26 BC, Augustus decided to assume overall command of his forces in Spain and established a large base near the River Esla, where three legions were stationed. During the following months, the Roman troops attacked the Astures again and gradually forced them to take refuge in their hill fort at Lancia, described as the most important stronghold of the Celtiberians by contemporary Roman historians. Before the legionaries could besiege them in Lancia, the Astures abandoned their fortification and moved to a nearby mountain known as Mons Medullius by the Romans, where they built a large encampment and prepared new defensive positions. The Roman legions besieged the Astures, building a 15-mile-long moat and ditch around the Celtiberian positions. Augustus wanted to trap his enemies and to prevent the Astures from being able to come down from the mountain in order to launch raids against the Roman positions. Understanding that their positions could

Roman legionary with *lorica segmentata* and leather pteruges. (*Photo and copyright by Legio XI C.P.F. Hispaniensis*)

Roman legionary wearing winter clothes in Celtic fashion under his armour. (*Photo and copyright by Legio XI C.P.F. Hispaniensis*)

not resist for long due to the lack of food and other supplies, the Astures chose to commit suicide en masse instead of surrendering. The Romans were shocked by such an act of desperate courage, the result of the Celtiberians' love of freedom. After the defeat of the Astures, the conflict continued for several more years, the Cantabrians still being determined to resist. The Romans experienced serious logistic difficulties and were never able to engage their enemies in a pitched battle. Augustus, who also had health problems during his time in Spain, had no choice but to use very harsh methods, with the Celtiberian civilians treated like enemy warriors and the territory of Cantabria looted with no mercy. The Cantabrians, in order to avoid slavery, often committed suicide when they were captured or surrounded. Consequently, the whole war was extremely violent and atrocities were committed by both sides. After ten years of campaigning, the major fighting came to an end in 19 BC with all the Cantabrian communities having been defeated by the Romans. Sporadic rebellions took place until 16 BC, but the emperor had practically pacified northern Spain and thus completed the conquest of Iberia. It should be noted, however, that two legions of the Roman Army (the X *Gemina* and the IV *Macedonica*) were left to garrison Asturias and Cantabria for the following seven decades due to the Romans' fear of further Celtiberian uprisings.

The next conflict in which Augustus was involved as princeps was the *Bellum Batonianum*, or Great Illyrian Revolt, which took place from AD 6–9 in the regions of Illyricum, Dalmatia and Pannonia. These areas corresponded more or less to the modern nations of Slovenia, Croatia and Hungary. The Roman Republic had conquered the western Balkans only with great difficulty after having fought three bloody wars against the local tribes of the Illyrians. These tribesmen, being extremely warlike, had resisted until 168 BC, when the Roman legions finally overcame them. The Illyrians had been the masters of the Adriatic Sea before the ascendancy of Rome, and were among the most feared pirates of Antiquity together with the Cilicians. The main cause behind the outbreak of the Illyrian Wars had been Rome's determination to destroy the naval power of the tribes living in the western Balkans. Although the Republic achieved its main objective, the Illyrian territories were never fully pacified by Rome. The conquerors initially ruled Illyricum as a protectorate, which was transformed into a *provincia pacata* during 27 BC. However, Augustus soon determined that Illyricum still needed a massive Roman military presence due to the possible outbreak of internal revolts; as a result, the region was transformed into a *provincia non pacata*. Before becoming emperor, as a young military commander, Augustus had already conducted a campaign in Illyricum. Indeed, the region had lived in a state of complete anarchy during most of the previous decades due to the ongoing Roman civil wars. The Illyrian pirates, never completely subdued by

Rome, had taken advantage of their masters' temporary weakness to conduct naval raids across the Adriatic and to attack the Roman military garrisons in the northern Balkans. Order was temporarily restored by the Romans before the outbreak of the civil war between Augustus and Mark Antony, but the whole area remained on the verge of revolt.

To secure a more direct control over the coastal areas where the pirates lived, Augustus decided to separate the coastal region of the western Balkans from the interior: the former became the new province of Dalmatia, while the latter continued to be known as Illyricum. Between 14 and 10 BC there were a series of minor rebellions in northern Dalmatia, during which the local tribes were supported by the peoples of Pannonia. The latter region was still independent from Rome and was inhabited by a mix of Illyrian and Celtic tribes; these, including also some Germanic elements, were very warlike and extremely hostile to Rome. After several more years of skirmishing and minor campaigns, the peoples of Illyria and Dalmatia finally decided to join their forces with those of the Pannonians to launch a large-scale insurrection against Rome. The Illyrian tribes from Illyricum and Dalmatia that formed an anti-Roman military alliance included the Daesitiatae, the Breuci, the Dalmatae, the Andizetes, the Pirustae, the Liburnians and the Iapydes. Both the Dalmatae and the Breuci were commanded by a warlord named Bato, and thus the new conflict became known as the *Bellum Batonianum*. The situation was an extremely difficult one for the Romans from the beginning, the revolting tribes having an efficient military organization that was partly modelled on the Roman one since thousands of the rebelling warriors had previously served in the Roman *auxilia* units. Like the Celtiberians, the Illyrians and Dalmatians always employed hit-and-run tactics against the Romans and avoided the fighting of pitched battles. Consequently, most of the Great Illyrian Revolt consisted of counter-insurgency operations carried on – with some difficulties – by the Romans.

In AD 6, Tiberius, the future successor of Augustus, asked the governor of Illyricum to join him in Germany with his military forces and to raise more auxiliary units from the Illyrians. These *auxilia*, once gathered, rebelled against the Romans and expelled them from their home province. Taking advantage of the Roman military weakness in that sector of the Empire, the rebels organized three separate armies: one was to invade Italy, another was to invade Macedonia and the third would remain in the western Balkans to prevent any future Roman counter-offensive. Augustus, greatly alarmed by these events, quickly started to gather substantial numbers of troops in order to stop an eventual Illyrian attack against Italy. Meanwhile, in Macedonia, the rebels obtained a series of successes until being stopped and defeated by the Thracians of the Odrysian Kingdom (a vassal state of the Roman Empire). Once

Roman legionary with *lorica segmentata*. (*Photo and copyright by Legio XI C.P.F. Hispaniensis*)

Roman legionary with *lorica segmentata* and decorative bronze disks. (*Photo and copyright by David Burns of Legio XIIII Gemina*)

enough soldiers were assembled, Tiberius marched on Illyricum with the objective of crushing the revolt, but he handled his forces passively and was not able to engage the enemy in any major battle. The war of attrition continued during AD 7, when the great military commander Germanicus was sent to help Tiberius with substantial reinforcements. The Romans, who now had three legions in the western Balkans, together with many auxiliary units, pushed back the rebels to the Claudian Mountains, located between northern Dalmatia and southern Pannonia, where a pitched battle was finally fought and won by Germanicus. The Roman forces were then divided into several detachments with the objective of chasing the bands of insurgents that were still active. The legionaries used very harsh repressive methods during this phase of the conflict, putting in practice the scorched earth strategy that had been sponsored by Tiberius. By AD 8, the civilians of both Dalmatia and Pannonia – ravaged by famine and disease – were ready to surrender, but were prevented from doing so by rebel warlords who wanted to continue fighting. The Dalmatians and Pannonians then turned against each other and the Pannonians finally decided to surrender. In AD 9, the Romans reconquered the whole of Dalmatia and decisively defeated the remaining rebels. With the end of the Great Illyrian Revolt, both Illyricum and Dalmatia were fully pacified, while the Romans also extended their sphere of influence over Pannonia. The latter was gradually occupied during the following years and was transformed into a new province in AD 14.

In 44 BC, at the time of Julius Caesar's assassination in the Senate, Gaul had been completely conquered by the Roman Republic, which now had a very long border with the lands inhabited by the Germani that were collectively known as Germania by the Romans. Until 30 BC, the military situation remained extremely quiet on the Rhine frontier, since the Romans were heavily involved in the civil wars that followed the death of Caesar. These ended only with the victory of Augustus, who emerged as the first emperor of Rome and gradually transformed the Republic into a Principate. During the years that saw the consolidation of Augustus' personal power, several of the Celtic tribes living in Gaul revolted against Rome and tried to restore their previous autonomy, but these local rebellions were all easily crushed by the Romans and peace reigned once again in Gaul by 27 BC. Augustus, however, was greatly irritated by the fact that the Celtic revolts had received material and ideological support from the Germanic tribes living on the eastern bank of the Rhine. As a result, he decided to secure the Roman military presence in the Rhineland by building new fortifications in the area and severely punishing all those Germani who had helped the Gallic rebels. Augustus was gradually developing the idea of *limes*, a fortified border. In his opinion, however, the Roman legions could have easily conquered most of Germania due to their military superiority. The emperor also believed that the cultural superiority of the Roman civilization would prove decisive against the Germani: in his view, the tribesmen had to be transformed from wild barbarians into civilized subjects of the Empire, as the Romans had already done with most of the Celts living in Gaul. During the long reign of Augustus, the Romans absorbed several small client kingdoms into the Empire by forming a social alliance with the local aristocracies. The nobles of the various protectorates were permitted to continue ruling over their countries but were required to send their sons to Rome in order for them to receive a perfect Roman education. Upon returning to their homeland, these client princes would be charged with the task of favouring the incorporation of their country into the Empire and would govern it as a province for Rome. Augustus also wanted to use this method of indirect conquest for Germania, but as we will see, his plans failed completely.

In 16 BC, the Romans were given the *casus belli* that they desired to initiate military operations in Germania. Three tribes living on the eastern bank of the Rhine had crossed the frontier and attacked the Roman units garrisoning the border. The Fifth Legion of the Roman Army was taken by surprise and defeated by the Germanic raiders, who were even able to capture its eagle (the most sacred insignia of a legion). This unexpected defeat convinced Augustus to transform Gaul into an immense military camp and to begin preparations for an invasion of Germania. The emperor felt that recent events had shown that Gaul could only be considered completely safe after the elimination of the menace represented by the Germani. The tribes that had been responsible for the raids and the Roman defeat were soon pushed back to the eastern bank of the Rhine, at which point they sent peace requests to Augustus. The emperor, however, was by now ready to implement his expansionistic policy towards Germania. Taxes were collected from every corner of Gaul to finance the upcoming military expedition, and a mint was established at Lugdunum (modern Lyon) in order to produce the money that was needed to pay the legionaries who were to operate in Germania. Drusus, a general with great combat experience and a stepson of Augustus, was made governor of Gaul in 13 BC; he would be the main commander of the Roman military forces tasked with invading Germania. Soon after his appointment, however, Drusus had to face a series of minor rebellions in Gaul, all of which were caused by the new taxation that had been recently imposed by the Romans. While crushing the Gallic revolts, Drusus also had to repulse a Germanic raid that erupted from the eastern bank of the Rhine, responding to this by launching a retaliatory attack across the river which caused significant losses to the Germani.

During 12 and 11 BC, Drusus operated in north-western Germany with great success, beginning by invading the land of the Usipetes and pillaging the territory of the Sicambri, two of the tribes that had attacked Gaul. He then moved to the

Roman legionary with crested helmet and *lorica segmentata*. (*Photo and copyright by David Burns of Legio XIIII Gemina*)

Roman legionary with bronze helmet and oval shield. (*Photo and copyright by David Burns of Legio XIIII Gemina*)

territory of present-day Netherlands, where the local Germanic communities of the Batavi and the Frisians were easily submitted. These soon became loyal clients of Rome, providing soldiers for the Roman *auxilia* units and even sending some chosen warriors who made up Augustus' private bodyguard. Augustus, as we have seen, was the creator of the Praetorian Guard and the other military corps that garrisoned the capital of the Empire. The emperor also established a small Germanic bodyguard – initially comprising 100 men but eventually becoming 500 strong – that was totally independent from the Praetorians: the *Germani corporis custodes*. This was entirely composed of Germanic warriors of the Batavian tribe, who protected the emperor and his family. Being foreigners, they were extremely loyal to Augustus and had no links with the political groups involved in the Roman power struggles. They were organized in *decuriae* (i.e. tens), each led by an officer known as a decurion. Having secured Roman dominance over the Batavi and the Frisians, Drusus moved along the northern coast of Germania and attacked the Chauci. After obtaining some other minor successes, he returned to Gaul due to the onset of winter. Within a few months, without experiencing any significant military difficulties, the Romans had occupied the territory of the Netherlands and had punished the most powerful Germanic tribes living near the Rhine for their incursions into Gaul.

During the following spring, Drusus launched another campaign in Germania. He rapidly subdued the Usipetes and then marched east in order to reach the River Weser. At this point the Romans were already in the very heart of Germania, home to the important tribe of the Cherusci. The Cherusci controlled a large portion of territory, which was located between the rivers Ems and Elbe. No Roman general had ever advanced so deeply into Germania, so Drusus was now moving in a completely unknown land. With the coming of winter, not being completely sure of the subdued Germani's loyalty towards the Empire, Drusus went back to Gaul without having submitted the Cherusci. During the retreat, the Romans were attacked by small parties of Germanic warriors, who harassed their columns with hit-and-run tactics. This caused significant losses to the legionaries, who were obliged to move very slowly on alien terrain. At that time the Rhine marked a frontier of civilizations between Gaul and Germania: in Gaul there were roads and *oppida* (fortified urban settlements) built by the Celts, while in Germania the population lived in isolated settlements and no roads existed. Most of the Germanic lands were covered by impenetrable forests, characterized by a very humid climate and the presence of swamps. The heavy-armoured Roman legionaries always had great difficulties in marching across Germania, since their slow columns and heavy equipment needed proper roads to move rapidly. In the spring of 10 BC, after having been elected consul, Drusus crossed back over the Rhine and returned with his troops into Germania, this time concentrating his efforts against the tribe of the Chatti, who lived south of the Germanic communities that had been subdued during the previous campaigns. Once again, the Romans were able to subdue the Germani and to obtain some local victories, but this new success of Drusus was not a decisive one. At the end of each Germanic campaign, the legionaries retreated back to Gaul without leaving behind any garrison that could control the newly submitted territories. In practice, the military campaigns of Drusus were mere demonstrations, aimed at transforming the Germanic leaders into vassal kings, rather than proper invasions with the intention of conquering new provinces and bringing stability to the region. The logistical difficulties experienced by the Romans prevented them from establishing a fixed military presence in Germania. All the gains obtained during each spring and summer were lost during the cold winter months, and thus the Germani could not be considered as submitted.

In 9 BC, Drusus began his fourth Germanic campaign, once more attacking the Chatti, who had not been completely submitted by the Romans during the previous conflict. This new campaign was particularly difficult for Drusus and his forces, who had to stop and fight several times during their march. The Romans reached the land of the Cherusci again and mounted a fresh attack on them with even greater numbers, which obliged the Germanic tribe to fall back to the River Elbe. The legions devastated most of the vast territory inhabited by the Cherusci, pillaging and looting with great violence. Drusus understood that the Cherusci were the strongest Germanic community in the central part of Germania and that by crushing their spirit, he would gain the respect of all the other tribes. With the Romans in close pursuit, and running the risk of being massacred, the Cherusci had no choice but to come to terms with Drusus. They recognized, at least formally, the suzerainty of Rome over their homeland. However, once again the Romans were obliged to leave Germania with the coming of winter, so their supremacy over the lands of the Cherusci could not be maintained. During his four Germanic campaigns, Drusus had been able to obtain several victories over the Germani: these, however, were more the result of his enemy's internal divisions than of his own military ability. The various Germanic tribes were extremely fragmented politically and spent most of their energy in bloody inter-tribal conflicts. As a result of this, the Romans could create alliances with individual tribes and use local rivalries to their advantage. By attacking the various Germanic communities one by one, the Romans always had a numerical superiority over their enemy and thus could prevail thanks to the perfect discipline of their legions. The campaigns of Drusus, however, had also shown the Romans all the dangers that could be encountered in Germania. It was an unknown and savage land, where the Roman Army could not fight with its usual tactics and where the terrain was an ally of the local populations. Drusus had been intelligent

Roman legionary wearing the *manica* and greaves introduced during the Dacian Wars. (*Photo and copyright by Legio XI C.P.F. Hispaniensis*)

Roman legionary with leather *manica*, bronze greaves and scale armour. (*Photo and copyright by David Burns of Legio XIIII Gemina*)

enough to follow Caesar's example and had used the tribal divisions of his opponents to obtain several victories, adopting the principle of *divide et impera* (divide and rule). Due to logistical difficulties, however, he had been obliged to abandon his conquest every year with the onset of winter, and thus up to this point the Roman presence in Germania remained a temporary one. On his way back to the Rhine at the end of his fourth Germanic campaign, Drusus fell from his horse and was badly wounded. His injury quickly became badly infected, and within a month the great Roman general died from the effects of gangrene.

Augustus, soon after hearing that Drusus was seriously ill, decided to send Tiberius to Germania as the new leader of the Roman troops operating across the Rhine. Tiberius, the brother of Drusus, did not at that stage of his career have any military experience, but he was extremely loyal to the emperor. In the opinion of Augustus, he would soon learn from experience. During 8 and 7 BC, Tiberius fought two campaigns in Germania, continuing what his brother had started. His efforts were mostly directed against the Sicambri, a tribe that put up a strong resistance against the Romans. Tiberius had to use all his military resources to defeat these warlike tribesmen, who used guerrilla tactics to slow down the advances of the legionaries and cause them significant losses. The Romans responded with harsh repressive methods, which included mass exterminations and the deportation of many Sicambri to the western bank of the Rhine. Tiberius was sure that these Germani would have just continued to revolt if the Romans had permitted them to remain in their homeland. After the end of Tiberius' second Germanic campaign, Roman propaganda presented western Germania as a pacified region of the Empire; this, however, was not true, as the subsequent military events on the eastern bank of the Rhine would show. Most of the Germanic tribes who had been defeated by the legions had accepted Roman supremacy only on paper, continuing to act as autonomous communities. In addition, the Romans had no fortifications and no significant garrisons in Germania that could control the territory and prevent the outbreak of rebellions. Some of the most important Germanic tribes living in the eastern part of Germania had not even been reached by the Romans, so most of Central Europe was still completely free from the political influence of the Empire.

Tiberius returned to Rome in 6 BC and was replaced as Roman commander on the Rhine by Lucius Domitius Ahenobarbus, who resumed the Roman offensives in Germania and rapidly moved east, crossing the River Elbe. Ahenobarbus, a skilled military commander, soon understood the importance of building an effective infrastructure in order to maintain a firm control over the Germanic territories. He ordered his military engineers to build causeways across all the bogs that could be found in the region between the Rhine and the Ems, which would enable the Roman legions to reach the Ems much more rapidly than before. The building of these *pontes longi*, which would soon be connected by a road according to Ahenobarbus' plans, was perceived as a clear act of hostility by the Cherusci who lived in the area. After establishing some permanent infrastructure, the Romans were able to deploy strong military garrisons in the region. Consequently, in 2 BC, the Cherusci rose up in revolt against the Romans and started to attack parties of legionaries that were patrolling their homeland. It should be noted, however, that not all members of the tribe were in favour of fighting a new war against Rome: while most of the common warriors hated the Romans and hoped to expel them from their homeland, some of the aristocracy were becoming increasingly interested in the new commercial possibilities offered by the arrival of the newcomers. The Rhine, after Julius Caesar's

Roman legionary with his full personal equipment. (*Photo by Marc Seriol [@marcmarkhus_photo] and copyright by Legio II Traiana Fortis – Cohors I Barcinonum, Barcino Oriens*)

conquest of Gaul, was not perceived as a real barrier by most of the peoples living on its shores, the great river being a waterway that connected different civilizations and that could be used to transport commercial products. The Romans had been trading with the Germani long before the ascendancy of Augustus, and now that they had a stronger presence on the western borders of Germania, many wealthy aristocrats of the Germanic tribes understood that they could become rich through trade. Certain products that could be found only in Germania, such as amber, were particularly

Roman legionary on the march, wearing a sun hat made of straw. (*Photo by Marc Seriol* [*@marcmarkhus_photo*] *and copyright by Legio II Traiana Fortis – Cohors I Barcinonum, Barcino Oriens*)

Rear view of a Roman legionary in full marching asset. (*Photo by Marc Seriol [@marcmarkhus_photo] and copyright by Legio II Traiana Fortis – Cohors I Barcinonum, Barcino Oriens*)

Roman legionary wearing the *subarmalis*, the protective padded garment worn under the metal armour. (*Photo and copyright by Legio XI C.P.F. Hispaniensis*)

Roman legionary wearing the *subarmalis*. (*Photo and copyright by Legio XI C.P.F. Hispaniensis*)

Roman legionary (left), officer of the auxiliaries (centre) and *Optio* (right). (*Photo and copyright by David Burns of Legio XIIII Gemina*)

interesting for the Romans; the same could be said for other goods, like wine, which were not produced in Germania but were loved by the Germani. Despite this, the great majority of the Cherusci was in favour of war against Rome, and thus hostilities commenced. Ahenobarbus, after contesting many minor battles, could not obtain a significant victory over the Cherusci, and therefore he was rapidly replaced by the Emperor. In 2 BC, Augustus sent another new military commander to Germania, the seasoned Marcus Vinicius.

Vinicius operated in Germania until AD 4 at the head of a considerable force that comprised five legions. He spent most of his years as commander of the Roman troops in Germania quelling local rebellions and marching across the Rhine to consolidate Rome's presence on the eastern bank of the great river. He obtained several victories, but none of them were truly decisive as the Germani always avoided facing the Romans in a major pitched clash. In AD 4, Augustus sent Tiberius to the

Rhine once again with orders to finally pacify the region once and for all. The future emperor performed extremely well during his second Germanic campaign, being able to subdue several minor tribes as well as to defeat the Cherusci who were still fighting against the Romans. According to Tiberius' propaganda, the Cherusci were completely pacified and thus they were given the honorific title of 'friends of the Roman People'. In reality, however, Tiberius established a formal alliance only with part of the tribe's nobility and not with the great majority of its warriors, who still hated the Romans and their culture. In AD 5, the Romans organized a major offensive in Germania, which began with a massive attack on the Chauci and continued with a rapid advance directed towards the heart of the Germanic territories. The Roman troops taking part in the offensive mostly advanced on land, but a portion of them was transported on a newly built river fleet. The various units then met on the banks of the Elbe, where Tiberius assembled them into a single army and made a strong demonstration of force in front of the Germani. After this, however, the Roman troops returned to their starting positions without leaving any garrison in Germania. Once again, the Roman Army had penetrated into the Germanic territories with a rapid offensive, but it had been unable to defeat the Germani in a pitched battle. During the retreat, as had happened many times before, the Romans were attacked by the Germanic warriors with hit-and-run tactics.

Chapter 3

The Battle of Teutoburg

The only positive result of the Roman demonstration of AD 5 was that the Cherusci, after years of internal divisions and of minor conflicts with the Romans, finally decided to become allies of Rome. This change of attitude was the result of an internal political struggle that saw a clash between those nobles of the Cherusci who wanted to establish a formal alliance with Rome and those who were opposed to such a move. The rapid campaign of Tiberius convinced the majority of the Cherusci that, at least for the moment, the Romans were too strong to be faced in a military confrontation. In addition, the Germani had understood that by trading with the Romans they could improve their living conditions and introduce some new products into their economy. The pro-Roman party of the Cherusci tribe was guided by a powerful family clan, whose members included a young aristocrat named Arminius. The latter was viewed by many as prince, since his father was one of the most important leaders of the Cherusci and one of the main supporters of the new pro-Roman policy. Tiberius supported the pro-Roman Cherusci and Arminius' clan in every possible way, in order to transform the Cherusci into Rome's most important Germanic allies. To sustain his local allies and to keep an eye on the Cherusci who still resented Roman rule, he built a stable winter base on the River Lippe. For the first time, the Romans now had a sizeable garrison in Germania. By AD 6, the Romans exerted some form of direct or indirect influence over the entire western part of Germania, with all the tribes living west of the River Elbe recognizing (at least formally) the supremacy of Rome. In south-eastern Germany, west of the Elbe, there was just one Germanic tribe that had not yet been submitted by the Romans: the Marcomanni, guided by their 'king', Maroboduus, who were without doubt the strongest of all the Germani from a military point of view. The Romans, having complete control over all the other Germanic communities, planned a massive pincer attack on the Marcomanni that would have involved an impressive total of twelve legions. Before this campaign could materialize, however, the Roman Army had to face the Great Illyrian Revolt, and the military forces assembled for the campaign against the Marcomanni had to be moved to the province of Illyricum. As a result, the Empire concluded a temporary peace treaty with the Marcomanni and recognized Maroboduus as their legitimate leader. Tiberius, who had guided the

Roman troops in Germania with great intelligence, assumed command of the forces fighting in the western Balkans, meaning that a new commander had to be chosen by Augustus in order to replace him. The emperor selected Publius Quintilius Varus.

At this point, before describing the events that would lead to the worst military defeat ever suffered by the Romans in Germania, it is important to understand who Arminius and Varus were. The Germanic prince, born in 18 or 17 BC, was the son of a powerful noble of the Cherusci tribe. Following Drusus' campaign against the Cherusci of 9 BC, he was sent to Rome as a hostage. As mentioned previously, Augustus wanted to apply in Germania his policy of cultural conquest that had already been employed successfully by the Romans with other client princes. By educating these princes in Rome and showing them the superiority of Roman civilization, the emperor hoped to obtain the peaceful submission of their homelands, with the princes returning to their nations to rule as vassals of Rome. Arminius was raised in Rome and educated as a perfect Roman boy: he entered the ranks of the Roman Army at a very young age and learned practically everything about the culture of Rome. Right from the beginning of his military career, Arminius demonstrated that he had great charisma and incredible personal capabilities. As a reward for his military services, he was granted Roman citizenship and was made part of the *equites* social class (inferior only to that of the senatorial aristocracy). During the Great Illyrian Revolt that broke out in AD 6, he served under Tiberius, commanding a unit of mounted *auxilia* that was made up of Germanic soldiers. Augustus was impressed by the loyalty and the combat skills of Arminius, who fought with distinction on several occasions during the Great Illyrian Revolt. As a result, the emperor ordered the Germanic prince to return to his homeland and to act as the personal aide of the new governor, Publius Quintilius Varus.

Varus came from a senatorial family of Rome and had been consul in 13 BC together with Tiberius, of whom he was a personal friend. He had married Vipsania, one of the daughters of Agrippa, who was Augustus' most trusted general and greatest friend. As a result of these connections, Varus had a brilliant career in the Roman administration despite being inept in many ways. While serving as the Roman governor of Syria from 7–4 BC, he soon showed all his personal limits: he had no respect for the traditions of the people living in his province, and his response to every problem was harsh repression. In addition, he increased taxes significantly and augmented his personal fortune by using illegal practices. In 4 BC, soon after the death of the local Roman client king Herod the Great, a popular revolt broke out in Judaea and Varus was forced to intervene with the four legions that were under his command in Syria. After occupying Jerusalem, he crushed the rebels with a violence that had never been seen before in Judaea: without any formal process, Varus crucified

Roman superior officer wearing parade helmet with mask and muscle cuirass. (*Photo and copyright by Legio XI C.P.F. Hispaniensis*)

Roman centurion wearing the distinctive helmet with transverse crest and muscle cuirass. (*Photo and copyright by Legio XI C.P.F. Hispaniensis*)

2,000 Jewish insurgents and committed a series of pointless atrocities. These events led to the development of a strong anti-Roman sentiment in Judaea and caused Varus' removal from the governorship of Syria. In AD 6, after a period of disgrace, Varus was appointed governor of Germania and was sent to the northern borders of the Empire. His main task was to organize the newly conquered lands into a proper Roman province in order to formalize their annexation to the Empire. Considering his personal background and previous career, Varus was not the right man to achieve such a difficult objective: he had little military experience, no knowledge of Germania and he was a terrible administrator. The governorship of Germania was a second chance for him and for his career, which he was able to obtain only thanks to his personal connections. Augustus knew all this very well, and thus decided to send Arminius to Germania in order to give Varus an expert and reliable adjutant.

When Varus arrived in Germania, the Roman troops deployed on the Rhine had been greatly reduced in number. Most the units stationed on the borders of Gaul had been sent to the western Balkans in order to fight against the local insurgents. As a result, only three legions were available for campaigning in Germania (the XVII, XVIII and XIX). These formations did not have a very long military tradition, since they had been formed during the last phase of the Roman civil wars. In addition, with the exception of the XIX, they had never fought for long periods in Germania. After returning to his homeland, Arminius soon became a trusted advisor to Varus, who knew practically nothing about Germania and had to rely on Arminius to take all the most important operational decisions. After a few months of governorship in Germania, Varus revealed he had learned very little from his previous mistakes by starting to impose a very heavy taxation on the Germanic tribes and using very harsh repressive methods to ensure the loyalty of his new subjects. The insolence and cruelty of Varus were intolerable for the Germani, who still considered themselves as free individuals who had accepted the Roman presence on their territories only for practical reasons. The taxes imposed by the new governor were impossible to sustain, while the violence of the occupiers caused the death of many civilians. In just a few months the Germani had lost their beloved freedom and had found themselves with an army of occupation in their homeland. Arminius was disgusted by the conduct of Varus and by his love for gold, gradually coming to the realization that the Germani could never flourish as a people under such an inept governor. He decided that it was better for them to be independent from Rome rather than being treated like animals. Despite having spent most of his life in Rome, the Germanic prince still loved his homeland and its inhabitants: Roman education had not cancelled his true Germanic spirit, as hoped by Augustus. The Romans had taught all their military practices to a man who was about to become one of their worst enemies. Learning from recent history, Arminius understood that the Germani had never been able to prevail against the Romans because they had always been fragmented politically and militarily. Now, with Varus in Germania, Arminius believed that the only way to defeat and expel the Romans was to create a large inter-tribal confederation of Germani that would be able to deploy a massive Germanic army.

Arminius had secret meetings with the leaders of the major Germanic tribes, at which he used his personal charisma to convince them of the necessity of creating a wide-ranging alliance. Most of the Germanic tribes were divided by strong rivalries, which made it difficult for Arminius to get them to forget their recent enmity as he proposed a new vision to all the Germani. Eventually, six major tribes of western Germania decided to support the plans of Arminius: the Cherusci, Marsi, Chatti, Bructeri, Chauci and Sicambri. These were supplemented by the surviving elements of the Suebi who still lived in Germania and had not been crushed by Caesar. After cementing the Germanic inter-tribal alliance, Arminius waited for the right moment to strike while continuing to act as Varus' main adjutant. In AD 9, during early September, Varus moved with his three legions from a newly built summer camp on the River Weser to his winter headquarters not far from the Rhine. During the march, Varus was informed of the outbreak of a local revolt that was taking place not far from his position. However, the reports of the rebellion were fabricated by Arminius, who wanted to move the legions from their usual path and make them enter a densely forested area where he could ambush them with his Germanic warriors. Varus, who had little knowledge of the terrain his legions were crossing, ordered Arminius to guide him to the location of the supposed rebellion. Arminius duly directed the Romans along a route that was totally unfamiliar for them. Another Cheruscan nobleman, a personal enemy of Arminius by the name of Segestes, tried to warn Varus about the possibility that the Roman legions could be ambushed, and even accused Arminius of being a traitor. Segestes' warnings, however, were dismissed by Varus, who felt they were merely the result of the feud between the two Cheruscan noblemen. Arminius then left the Roman column under the pretext of assembling some Germanic forces that would support the Romans in crushing the uprising.

In reality, the Cheruscan leader went to the defensive positions that his Germanic warriors had prepared in the surrounding woods and assumed command of his forces. The ambush organized by Arminius took place at Kalkriese Hill, in Lower Saxony, not far from the present-day town of Detmold. Varus' troops comprised not only the three legions but also six infantry *cohortes* and three cavalry *alae* of auxiliaries. These, like most of the legionaries, did not have much combat experience. The Roman soldiers did not march in combat formation, since they were convinced they were moving through safe territory where they would not be attacked. The

Roman centurion with *lorica hamata*. (*Photo by Marc Seriol [@ marcmarkhus_photo] and copyright by Legio II Traiana Fortis – Cohors I Barcinonum, Barcino Oriens*)

Roman centurion wearing *phalerae* decorative disks. (*Photo by Marc Seriol* [*@marcmarkhus_photo*] *and copyright by Legio II Traiana Fortis – Cohors I Barcinonum, Barcino Oriens*)

various military units were also interspersed with several hundred civilian camp followers, which included the families of the legionaries and the auxiliaries, as well as merchants and other workers who lived with the soldiers in their camps. In total the Roman force comprised around 19,000 soldiers, who marched together with 4,000–5,000 non-combatants. Following Arminius' directions, the Roman column started to follow a path that crossed a densely forested area, and as they continued to advance, the path became increasingly narrow and muddy. Expecting no attacks from the local tribes, Varus did not send any cavalry explorers ahead of his main column and continued to march even after a violent storm began. The Roman column was gradually becoming dangerously long and too slow due to the broken morphology of the land that it was crossing. By now it was around 20km long, so the units marching at the head of it could not easily communicate with those at the back. When the legions were thus stretched and dispersed through the woods, the Germanic warriors of Arminius emerged from the dense vegetation of the forest and started to attack the Romans. The Romans were taken totally by surprise, and had no time to deploy themselves in defensive formation; in any case, the limited space available along the narrow path they were following made the adoption of any combat formation practically impossible. Arminius, with his extensive knowledge of Roman tactics, had chosen the perfect location to stage his ambush. He ordered his warriors not to attack the Romans directly, at least during the early phase of the battle, but instead to skirmish with the legionaries from a distance by using their light javelins. In these opening exchanges of the clash, hundreds of Romans were killed without even seeing their enemies.

The Germani attacked individual sections of the long Roman column, so they always had a decisive local superiority over their enemies. Any small group of legionaries who became isolated from the main column was rapidly surrounded by the Germanic warriors and massacred. By the end of the first day of battle, the Romans had already lost thousands of soldiers without causing any significant losses to their enemies. In heavy rain, Varus ordered the construction of a temporary camp in the forest and spent the night in this newly fortified position. On the following morning, the Romans tried to leave the woods and reach an open area that was located not far from their temporary camp, but the legionaries were attacked again by Arminius' men and were not able to get out of the forest. The torrential rain at this time did not help the Romans, who were by now experiencing real panic and had no idea how to deal with the situation they were facing. At the end of the second day of battle, the Romans marched by night towards the foot of Kalkriese Hill in the hope of deploying on some higher ground and putting up a stronger resistance against the Germani. Arminius, however, had already foreseen this move and prepared a strong

Roman centurion with scale armour and rectangular shield. (*Photo and copyright by Legio XI C.P.F. Hispaniensis*)

Roman centurion with scale armour and greaves. (*Photo and copyright by Legio XI C.P.F. Hispaniensis*)

defensive position at Kalkriese Hill. To reach the hill, the Romans had to abandon the main path and follow a narrow sandy strip between the hill and a nearby swamp that was known as the Great Bog. Between Kalkriese Hill and the Great Bog there was a small gap of only 100 metres, which had dense vegetation on the left at the foot of the hill. Upon reaching this location, the Romans saw that the new path was blocked by a trench which made it impossible for them to reach the top of the hill. Meanwhile, they learned that the Germani had built a solid earthen wall in the dense vegetation that covered the foot of Kalkriese Hill on their left. This, located close to the road, permitted the Germani to attack the Romans with their throwing weapons from behind cover. Arminius had prepared what many have described as the most perfect ambush in the history of the Ancient World: Varus and his men had no possibility of escape. To the rear, the Roman column had 10,000 Germanic warriors who had followed it and were ready to prevent any retreat, while to their front, the narrow path that they had been following disappeared in the forest, where the vegetation was too dense to permit any further advance. On their right, the Romans had the Great Bog, while on their left, there was the earthen wall built by Arminius and defended by over 14,000 Germanic warriors.

The Germani attacked the Romans with increasing violence, killing hundreds of them without having to come out from their fortified positions. The legionaries made a desperate attempt to storm the earthen wall, but were repulsed with severe losses. At this point, the few cavalry of the Roman column tried to flee from the trap by abandoning the foot troops, but the mounted *auxilia* were soon intercepted and massacred by the larger force of Germanic cavalry that Arminius had kept in reserve. When it became apparent that the Roman formations were collapsing, the Germani came out from their positions and launched a direct attack against the surviving legionaries. The ensuing hand-to-hand fighting was particularly violent, the Roman soldiers having no chance of survival and only being able to save their honour by putting up a heroic last stand. Varus, realizing that the disaster was the result of his ineptitude, committed suicide, while his soldiers grouped themselves in various improvised defensive formations and tried to resist as long as they could. They were attacked by thousands of Germani, who slaughtered them one by one, together with all the civilians who were part of the Roman column. Most of the Roman officers committed suicide, preferring that to capture and torture. In total, more than 20,000 Romans were killed in the clash, that would become known as the Battle of the Teutoburg Forest. It was one of the worst defeats ever suffered by the Roman Army, which lost three of its formidable legions in an obscure and unknown forest in Central Europe. The few surviving Romans were all captured and enslaved by the Germani, except for the officers, who were sacrificed during the religious

Roman centurion with scale armour and parade javelin. (*Photo and copyright by Marilyn Paléri of the historical reconstitution association Lorica Romana*)

Roman centurions wearing *lorica segmentata*. (*Photo and copyright by Legio XI C.P.F. Hispaniensis*)

ceremonies that celebrated the great Germanic victory. Only a very few Romans were ransomed and could return to the western bank of the Rhine, where they reported the terrible events of Teutoburg.

Arminius, in obtaining a complete victory over the Romans, had practically destroyed all the Imperial military forces that were deployed in Germania. His warriors took thousands of weapons and pieces of armour from the dead legionaries and auxiliaries, in addition to the goods and money transported by the civilians who were part of the Roman column. When news of the Battle of Teutoburg reached the Rhine, the Roman authorities had no choice but to evacuate all the forts and garrisons that had been recently built on the eastern bank of the river, leaving the territory of Gaul exposed to raids by the Germani. Only one Roman fort, built at Aliso, resisted for several weeks, repulsing all the attacks launched by the Germani. Although its garrison was eventually forced to retreat back to the Rhine like all the other Roman units, it had gained enough time to enable the legions that were stationed in Gaul to organize a defensive line along the river. At that moment the Romans had just two legions on the frontier between Gaul and Germania, which made Rome fear an invasion of Gallic territory by Arminius. The Germanic leader, however, was fully satisfied with having achieved his primary objective: freeing the whole territory of Germania from Roman military presence. Upon hearing of the terrible defeat suffered in Germania, Augustus was so shocked that he was reported to have spent several days and nights butting his head against the walls of his palace. According to the Roman historian Suetonius, the Emperor continued desperately shouting '*Quintili Vare, legiones redde!*', which translates as 'Quintilius Varus, give me back my legions!' Augustus spent the last five years of his life thinking of the massacre caused by the ineptitude of Varus, which became commonly known in Rome as the *Clades Variana* (the Varian disaster). The three legions that had been destroyed by Arminius were never reformed, the Romans being extremely superstitious and not wanting to give a new military unit the official denomination of a corps that had been wiped out in such terrible circumstances.

After the Battle of Teutoburg, Arminius became the supreme leader of western Germania and also increased his influence over those Germanic tribes that had not been part of his confederation. The Cheruscan leader considered his victory over the Romans to be only the starting point of a larger process that would end with the political unification of Germania. Arminius, however, knew very well that the Romans would soon attack the Germani in a bid to have their revenge: they would assemble a large invading force and would avoid the mistakes committed by Varus. Attempting to establish a military alliance with the powerful Marcomanni, whose leader Maroboduus was the only other supreme overlord of Germania, Arminius sent them the severed head of Varus together with the offer of an anti-Roman

Roman centurion with lorica segmentata and rectangular shield. (*Photo and copyright by Legio XI C.P.F. Hispaniensis*)

Roman centurion with winter marching dress. (*Photo and copyright by Legio XI C.P.F. Hispaniensis*)

alliance. Maroboduus, who had recently been recognized as king of his tribe by the Romans, refused Arminius' offer and instead sent Varus' head to Rome to show his respect for the Empire. Meanwhile, the Romans sent Tiberius with three legions to Gaul to prepare for a massive counter-offensive: the honour of the Roman Army had been offended and the imperial eagles of Varus' legions were in enemy hands. The Marcomanni remained neutral during the ensuing conflict between Arminius and the Romans, meaning the Cheruscan leader had to fight alone against a superior force. From a historical point of view, the Battle of Teutoburg had an enormous importance, since it marked the end of the short-lived Roman presence in Germania. Following Arminius' victory, the Rhine started to mark the border between two worlds and two civilizations: those of the Romans and the Germanic peoples. This cultural division of Europe is still visible today, in the languages spoken by the European peoples and in their way of thinking. No one knows how the history of Europe may have been different if present-day Germany had also been 'romanized'. But what we can say is that the later Germanic invasions of the Roman Empire would have never taken place, and that the fall of Rome would have been completely different from the one we know (which was mostly the result of the great Germanic migrations).

Chapter 4

The Consolidation of the Borders

Following the Battle of Teutoburg, Germania was in turmoil. The western part of the region was dominated by Arminius, who was now waiting for the return of the Romans seeking revenge, whereas the eastern portion was dominated by the Marcomanni, who had transferred their communities to the territories of the present-day Czech Republic. As we have seen in the previous chapter, soon after achieving his great victory over the Romans, Arminius had tried to form an alliance with the Marcomannic king Maroboduus, but the latter had refused. This political act, unexpected by Arminius, led to a progressive increase in tension between the Cherusci and the Marcomanni. Germania could not be ruled by two overlords, but for the moment the inter-tribal wars were postponed in view of the imminent return of the legions of Rome. Augustus was furious at the *Clades Variana*, and soon after the events at Teutoburg he had sent Tiberius, together with significant military forces, to Germania. Apparently, the emperor wanted to attempt a reconquest of the areas that had been lost, but Tiberius had other plans for the Germanic campaign that he was about to conduct. Indeed, upon reaching the Rhine in AD 10, Tiberius decided to simply stabilize the eastern frontier of Gaul and made no attempt to crush Arminius' forces in their own territory. The Rhine fortifications were repaired and supplemented by new defensive structures, with the available garrison forces distributed in a more effective way and the whole frontier region being militarized. After securing his supply lines, Tiberius moved into Germania, but only to conduct punitive long-range raids, the Romans burning houses, devastating fields and routing all the local Germanic forces that tried to stop them. Arminius, understanding that the Romans had decided not to attempt a new invasion, remained on the defensive and did not attack the raiders. Tiberius moved very slowly during this new campaign in Germania and took all necessary precautions: he was terrified about the possibility of being ambushed like Varus, and thus did not deploy a very adventurous strategy. His advances were extremely cautious, all orders were given in writing and he had to be consulted for any decision (even the smallest ones), Tiberius being obsessed by the fear that a traitor could cause the defeat of his forces.

In AD 14, Augustus died and Tiberius went back to Rome in order to become emperor. His military actions in Germania over recent years had achieved very

Roman centurion mounted on his horse. (*Photo and copyright by Legio XI C.P.F. Hispaniensis*)

little, except for punishing some local communities that had supported Arminius. Command of the Roman troops on the Rhine then passed to Nero Claudius Drusus, the adoptive son of Tiberius, who was nicknamed Germanicus because of the great victories he went on to achieve in Germania. Germanicus was the son of Drusus, who had been one of the first Roman generals campaigning in Germania (as we have seen in an earlier chapter). Drusus was a younger brother of Tiberius, who was thus the uncle of Germanicus. The second emperor of Rome had a predilection for his adoptive son Germanicus, to the point of choosing him as his successor instead of his own son, Drusus Iulius Caesar. Germanicus was much more aggressive than Tiberius from the beginning of his period of command in Germania, and soon earned an excellent military reputation. He lived together with his soldiers and faced all the same difficulties encountered by his men; for these reasons and for his simple way of life he was particularly loved by the legionaries. With an impressive force of twelve legions under his command, during the years AD 14–16 Germanicus attacked the confederation of Arminius and obtained a series of brilliant victories. The new Roman commander did not want to invade Germania, since such an act was by now considered impossible by all Romans. He wanted, instead, to fight a great pitched battle against the Germani in order to crush them and eradicate the terrible memories of Teutoburg from the hearts of the Romans. Germanicus had two further objectives: to find the three imperial eagles that had been captured from Varus' legions and to kill Arminius. The Romans understood that with the death of the Cheruscan leader, the partial unity of the Germani would soon end. The divided Germanic tribes may have remained impossible to conquer, but they would have been in no position to menace the frontiers of the Empire (at least for the moment).

Germanicus mounted a rapid offensive and attacked the lands of the Chatti and the Cherusci. He went to the site of the Battle of Teutoburg and buried the bones of the Roman soldiers that still lay on the ground there several years after the massacre. This act was extremely important from a symbolic point of view, especially for the morale of the Roman Army. During this early phase of his three-year Germanic campaign, Germanicus was also able to find one of the three imperial eagles for which he was searching. The Germani did not try to stop the movements of the legions, simply conducting some minor skirmishes to harass their enemy. As time progressed, however, Arminius was forced to change his strategy, as the Roman legions were destroying and pillaging everything they encountered on their march and this was damaging his personal reputation as overlord of the Germanic confederation. Many of the tribes who had followed him with enthusiasm were now ready to rebel against his rule, so he was left with no choice but to fight against Germanicus in a pitched battle. This took place at Idistaviso, on the right bank of the River Weser, between present-day Minden and Hamelin. Arminius deployed his forces in an intelligent way, ensuring that between him and the legions was the Weser: he was on the right bank, Germanicus the left bank. Crossing the river under a rain of missile weapons thrown by the Germani would have been extremely difficult for the legions. Germanicus, however, could count on large contingents of mounted

Roman centurion with summer marching dress. He is carrying the *vitis*, the peculiar vine staff of centurions. (*Photo and copyright by Legio XI C.P.F. Hispaniensis*)

Roman cavalryman with parade helmet and greaves (left), and *Optio* with crested helmet and scale armour (right). (*Photo and copyright by Legio XIIII Gemina*)

auxiliaries from Gaul and some communities of Germanic allies (the Batavi and the Chauci) who had joined the Roman Army. Covered by the cavalry, which advanced in two columns, the bulk of the Roman forces were able to cross the Weser without experiencing major difficulties. One of the two Roman cavalry columns, mostly made up of Batavi, advanced deeply against the enemy positions and lost contact with the rest of Germanicus' troops. Finding themselves surrounded by the Cherusci, they risked being completely destroyed. Eventually, however, the column managed to link up with the rest of the Roman cavalry and was able to retreat to safety. The main Germanic army, commanded by Arminius, left its initial positions after being unable to stop the Roman crossing of the Weser. During the night that followed the first day of battle, the Romans built a large fortified camp in the centre of the battlefield. The Germani attacked this structure, hoping to be helped by the darkness, but all their assaults were repulsed. The decisive clash between the two armies took place on the following morning. The Germani attacked first, but they were repulsed with very high casualties. At this point of the battle, the two Roman wings, made up of cavalry and auxiliaries, encircled the enemy and attacked it on the flanks. Arminius, seriously wounded, was left with no choice but to flee from the battlefield with the few survivors of his army in order to escape capture. The Battle of Idistaviso had been Germanicus' masterpiece, proving that the Roman Army was still invincible on the open field: Arminius had been no match for it.

Following their victory, the Romans occupied a strong defensive position that had been built by the local Germanic tribes not far from the battlefield. This structure, known as the Angrivarian Wall, marked the border between the territories of the Angrivarii and those of the Cherusci. Expecting a Germanic counter-attack, Germanicus occupied the wall and waited for the arrival of the enemy. The Germani duly attacked the earthen wall shortly after the Romans occupied it, but all their assaults were repulsed with severe losses. After this second defeat, Arminius could no longer counter the actions of the Romans in Germania and was forced to deal with the rapid crumbling of the multi-tribal confederation that he had forged. The lands of the Chatti and the Marsi were devastated by Germanicus, who managed to find another imperial eagle of the three lost at Teutoburg. After having achieved all their objectives except for the capture of Arminius, the Romans went back to the Rhine and once again left Germania without attempting an occupation of the territory. Their revenge had been cruel and had destroyed any possibility of Germanic political unity. In AD 17, hoping to take advantage of Arminius' weakness, the Marcomanni of Maroboduus attacked the Cherusci. This inter-tribal war, which was probably instigated by the Romans, ended in a stalemate, with the Marcomanni unable to achieve any significant victory. A few years later, both the main protagonists of the

Roman *Optio* with scale armour. (*Photo and copyright by Legio XIIII Gemina*)

Battle of Idistaviso died: Germanicus was poisoned by his opponents in AD 19, while he was in Antioch, while Arminius was assassinated two years later by a rival nobleman of his own Cheruscan tribe. With the death of Arminius, any hope of Germanic political unity vanished. The great warrior leader had, however, prevented forever the possibility that the Romans could conquer Germania. In AD 18, meanwhile, Maroboduus was replaced as king of the Marcomanni by a younger noble who was backed by the Romans, and would die as an exile, in Italy, in AD 37.

As anticipated above, the latter years of Augustus' reign and those of Tiberius' early reign saw the Romans also consolidating their presence in Pannonia (modern-day Hungary). This region had great strategic importance, being located north of the western Balkans, where several important commercial routes connected the western territories of the Empire with those in the east. After the death of Julius Caesar, the Pannonians, hoping to gain some advantage from the chaotic political situation in Rome at the time, had supported an Illyrian revolt and had defeated – together with their allies – the Roman garrisons stationed in Illyricum. Between 35 and 33 BC, to restore order in the area, a young Augustus (at that time not yet emperor) campaigned against both the Pannonians and the Illyrians. The first Roman incursions into Pannonia were conducted during this conflict, and the southern portion of the country came under a strong Roman influence (albeit not being permanently occupied). From 17–16 BC, the Celts of northern Pannonia allied themselves with the Kingdom of Noricum, located on the western border of their territories, and resumed hostilities against Rome. The Kingdom of Noricum was originally inhabited by several Celtic tribes, which were gradually unified into a federal state that was under the strong influence of Rome. The Celts of Noricum had strong political and commercial relations with those living in Pannonia and with the other Celtic tribes settled in Switzerland. Noricum was in a delicate geographical position, with Roman Italy to the south and the fierce Germanic nations to the north. As a result, its political leaders had no choice but to form an alliance with the Roman Republic in order to obtain its military protection.

The Kingdom of Noricum was created around 150 BC, since when it had provided the Romans with large amounts of excellent weapons. Celtic Austria was famous for the high quality production of metal weapons and tools. Noricum was rich in iron, gold and salt: both the Romans and the Germani badly needed these natural resources, and thus the local Celts had to maintain some kind of equilibrium in order to preserve their independence. Noric steel was particularly appreciated for its quality and hardness, with most of the weapons used to equip the Roman legions being manufactured from it. During the opening phase of Tiberius' reign, the Austrian Celts decided to change their attitude towards Rome and joined their Pannonian

Roman *Optio* with crested helmet. (*Photo and copyright by David Burns of Legio XIIII Gemina*)

cousins in an invasion of Roman Macedonia. The venture, however, was a complete failure: the invaders were promptly defeated and – in retaliation – the Roman legions invaded the Kingdom of Noricum (annexing it to the Empire). The northern part of Pannonia remained independent, even after these campaigns. In 14 BC, the Illyrians of southern Pannonia rebelled against Roman rule, with the help of the Celts living in the northern part of the country. The new war raged until 10 BC and ended with the Roman reconquest of southern Pannonia, while some northern territories of the Celts were also occupied by the legions. Roman dominance in the region was becoming absolute, and the only chance for the Celts and Illyrians to survive was to unite against the common menace in order to regain some form of independence. As we have seen, these last hopes for freedom were crushed during the Great Illyrian Revolt. Pannonia became a Roman province in AD 14, just a few years after order was completely restored in both Illyricum and Dalmatia.

Roman *Optio* wearing *lorica segmentata*. He is carrying the *hastile*, or wooden staff, that was peculiar of his rank. (*Photo by Marc Seriol* [@ *marcmarkhus_photo*] *and copyright by Legio II Traiana Fortis – Cohors I Barcinonum, Barcino Oriens*)

Roman *Optio* with *lorica segmentata*. (*Photo and copyright by Legio XI C.P.F. Hispaniensis*)

During the first decades of the Imperial period, the Roman Army was involved in several minor military operations in Thrace and in Dacia; the eastern Balkans, in fact, were still mostly free from Rome's political and military influence. In 150 BC, an attempt to re-establish an independent Kingdom of Macedonia provoked the outbreak of the Fourth Macedonian War, which lasted until 148 BC. During this conflict, like in several previous ones, the Thracians were part of the anti-Roman alliance. The pretender to the Macedonian throne, however, was defeated by the Roman Republic, and Macedonia was officially transformed into a Roman province in 146 BC. From that year, a state of constant war existed on the border between Roman Macedonia and independent Thrace. The Romans were determined to transform the various Thracian tribes into client communities, and considered themselves to be the heirs of Macedonia's political influence over Thrace. The Thracians, who had no intention of accepting the Romans as their overlords, soon started to launch aggressive raids against the province of Macedonia. During the many minor wars fought against the Thracians, the Roman Army was defeated on several occasions, even having one of its proconsuls killed. The Thracian warriors, with their elusive skirmishing tactics and great mobility, proved very difficult opponents for the Romans, who did not have an extensive knowledge of the eastern Balkans.

From 146 BC, the Roman Republic tried to recreate some sort of unified Thracian state in order to transform the region into one of its vassal kingdoms. However, it would have been much easier for the Romans to control a single puppet kingdom rather than keeping order among many warlike tribes. Around 100 BC, a new Odrysian Kingdom was established, but this did not last for long due to the internal divisions of the Thracians (most of whom were strongly against Rome's indirect rule of their homeland). Around 30 BC, some form of Thracian Kingdom had been restored by the Romans, and the Thracian tribes that were still autonomous had all accepted some form of Roman suzerainty. In 15 BC, the population of the Thracian Kingdom rose in revolt against the Romans and killed the puppet monarch who had been chosen by Rome, but the rebellion was swiftly crushed by the legions. New Thracian uprisings took place during the following decades as the Roman presence in present-day Bulgaria became increasingly stable. In AD 12, the Romans divided the territories of Thrace into two puppet kingdoms, but this measure failed to change the situation. The two Thracian realms soon started to fight against each other and anti-Roman uprisings continued with great frequency. In AD 45, a major new rebellion erupted in Thrace, which caused the death of one of the puppet kings chosen by the Romans. At this point, to stop the endemic guerrilla fighting that was ravaging the region, Emperor Claudius (the fourth ruler of Rome, after Augustus, Tiberius and Caligula) decided to transform Thrace into a Roman province in AD 46. Thracian uprisings and revolts

Roman *Optio* with crested helmet. (*Photo and copyright by Legio XI C.P.F. Hispaniensis*)

continued for several years, but without achieving significant results. Like many other peoples living around them, the Thracians had lost forever their independence and were already slowly disappearing from history. During the following centuries, they would be a fundamental component of the Roman Empire's population.

As a result of the Celtic migrations across Europe, the Celtic presence in Dacia (modern Romania) soon became quite significant during the second half of the third century BC, but the newcomers always had to co-exist with the local population, as the nomadic Scythians had done before them. This situation continued until 150 BC, when the Dacians started to fight against the Celtic communities living on their territories in a bid to expel them from Transylvania. This was not a simple process, the Celts having established themselves very firmly in Dacia, but the Dacians were supported in their long struggle by the powerful Thracian tribe of the Getae (who controlled a portion of territory located north of the Danube). The violent conflict between Dacians and Celts came to a critical point around 60 BC, when a great war leader emerged from the tribes of Dacia: Burebista. He guided the Dacians in the decisive moment of the conflict against the Celts, whom they expelled from the middle Danube region. Soon after achieving his objectives, Burebista was crowned as overlord of the Dacians and started to unify all the tribes of his people into a centralized state. This confederation developed quite rapidly, thanks to the great personal capability of

Roman *Optio* in full marching asset, with sun hat. (*Photo and copyright by Legio XI C.P.F. Hispaniensis*)

Roman *Optio* drinking from his canteen made of leather. (*Photo and copyright by Legio XI C.P.F. Hispaniensis*)

Burebista, who ordered the construction of a system of hill forts across Dacia in order to control the territories of the various communities and gradually absorbed the powerful Getae into his political sphere of influence. Until 40 BC, he continued to fight on the borders of his new state against the Celtic Boii, who still represented a potential menace for Dacia and continued to launch raids against Burebista's lands. Burebista, after having secured his control over most of the eastern Balkans, started to have an aggressive attitude towards Roman Macedonia and launched several raids against the Illyrian and Thracian tribes living on his southern borders. From 55 BC, the Dacians also started to attack the Greek colonies that were established on the Black Sea coastline. The Romans did very little to obstruct Dacian expansionism during this phase because they were heavily involved on other fronts: Julius Caesar was completing the conquest of Gaul and there was a growing possibility of a civil war between him and Pompey.

This internecine conflict eventually erupted in 49 BC and went on to affect the whole Mediterranean, with each state bordering the Roman Republic being forced to take up a position in favour of either Caesar or Pompey. Burebista decided to support Pompey, but the latter was defeated and killed before he could send any military contingent into Roman Macedonia. Caesar was well aware of the Dacians' military potential and considered Burebista as a dangerous enemy. Indeed, after becoming the sole ruler of Rome, Caesar started planning a major punitive expedition against Dacia, but he was assassinated in 44 BC before the planned campaign could become reality. Several months after the death of Julius Caesar, Burebista was also killed during a plot against him, organized by members of the Dacian aristocracy, who resented the new centralized form of government introduced by Burebista and feared the possibility of an armed conflict with Rome. Soon after these events, the Dacian Kingdom collapsed and was broken up into several smaller realms, and these soon started to quarrel between themselves. Following Burebista's death, the Dacians no longer represented a menace for the Romans. Their large kingdom was now fragmented into several parts and the great multi-national army created by Burebista (numbering around 100,000 warriors) no longer existed. Consequently, the Roman Republic abandoned Caesar's plans for an invasion of Dacia and limited itself to keeping order on the Balkan frontier. This situation started to change only in AD 69 with the emergence of a new Dacian leader, named Duras.

Until the end of Augustus' reign in AD 14, Dacia continued to be divided into five smaller kingdoms that could all be easily controlled by the Romans. In the following decades, however, a new sense of national identity started to emerge among the Dacian communities. The Romans were increasingly perceived as a deadly menace, meaning that all the Dacians began feeling the need for joint action against them. Duras became king in AD 69, after his father Scorilo was probably killed during a first Dacian raid launched against the Roman province of Moesia. The latter had been created by the Romans during the reign of Augustus as a buffer zone between Macedonia and Dacia. Moesia was located to the north of Macedonia and the south-west of Dacia. Before the Romans' arrival, this region was inhabited by the Moesi (a tribe of Dacian stock), the Triballi (a Thracian tribe) and a portion of the Germanic Bastarnae. The Romans considered Moesia to be a key region and decided they had to conquer it in order to protect Macedonia from the incursions of the barbarians living north of the Danube. The northern border of the new province was to be marked by the course of the great river. The *casus belli* for the invasion of Moesia was provided to the Romans by the Bastarnae, who attacked one of their allied Thracian tribes.

Roman *Tesserarius*, with the small block of wood on which watchwords were written. (*Photo by Marc Seriol [@marcmarkhus_photo] and copyright by Legio II Traiana Fortis – Cohors I Barcinonum, Barcino Oriens*)

Roman *Vexillifer* with scale armour. (*Photo and copyright by Marilyn Paléri of the historical reconstitution association Lorica Romana*)

During the ensuing conflict, thousands of Bastarnae were killed by the Romans and the Moesi were forced to submit. Before more reinforcements sent by the northern Bastarnae could come south of the Danube, the Romans had already completed the conquest of Moesia, which was transformed into one of their provinces in AD 6. The Dacians, who never accepted Rome's conquest of Moesia, soon started to attack the region with a series of rapid incursions. The first major raid, carried out by Scorilo in AD 69, ended in failure. For the moment, however, the Romans had no intention of fighting a large-scale war against the Dacians, and so they continued to adopt a defensive strategy on the Danubian *limes*.

During most of the late Hellenistic period, which corresponded to the military ascendancy of Republican Rome, Anatolia – modern Turkey, known as Asia Minor by the Romans – saw the presence of three small political entities that co-existed with the Roman province of Asia: the Kingdom of Bithynia, the Kingdom of Cappadocia and Galatia. The Bithynians were one of the Thracian tribes that had migrated from Europe to Anatolia, just like the more numerous Phrygians. Despite being formally subjects of the Persian Empire, from 435 BC (well before the arrival of Alexander the Great) they had started to act as an independent realm. After 297 BC, the rulers of Bithynia started to call themselves kings, becoming fully autonomous in 281 BC. Nicomedes I, ascending to the Bithynian throne in 280 BC, was the first monarch to launch a significant process of hellenization in his realm, adopting phalangite tactics. Until then, the Bithynians had continued to fight as light infantrymen like every Thracian tribe. In 74 BC, the last monarch of Bithynia, having no heirs, bequeathed his kingdom to Rome. The independent Kingdom of Cappadocia was founded in 331 BC by Ariarathes, the last Persian governor of the Cappadocian Satrapy. Since the Macedonians continued their advance towards the heart of the Persian Empire without attacking Cappadocia, Ariarathes was able to retain power in his own province and avoided a direct confrontation with the army of Alexander the Great. Nevertheless, Ariarathes was defeated and killed by one of Alexander's successors in 322 BC, but after a brief period of Macedonian occupation, Cappadocia became again independent in 301 BC under Ariarathes' son. The latter initiated a new royal family that was to last until 96 BC, when Mithridates VI of Pontus invaded Cappadocia and briefly annexed it to his possessions. After having defeated Mithridates, the Romans decided to install a new royal family in Cappadocia and transformed the small realm into a client kingdom. In 36 BC, the last exponent of this new dynasty died without heirs and thus the Romans gave Cappadocia to a local noble named Archelaus, who was a personal friend of Mark Antony. When Archelaus died in AD 17, Cappadocia was absorbed into the Roman Empire.

When the Celts invaded the southern Balkans in 280 BC, a number of them crossed the Hellespont and entered Anatolia. Apparently, the Celtic invaders came to Asia at

Roman *Vexillifer* wearing *lorica segmentata*. (*Photo by Marc Seriol* [@ *marcmarkhus_photo*] *and copyright by Legio II Traiana Fortis – Cohors I Barcinonum, Barcino Oriens*)

Roman *Signifer* wearing scale armour. (*Photo and copyright by Legio XI C.P.F. Hispaniensis*)

the invitation of Nicomedes I, King of Bithynia, who wanted their military help in a dynastic struggle against his brother. The Celts who settled in the centre of Anatolia belonged to three different tribes: the Tectosages, the Trocmi and the Tolistobogii. These settled in the plateau of Phrygia, after submitting the local inhabitants of Thracian descent, and this region, where the modern city of Ankara is located, soon started to be known as Galatia. The three tribes organized themselves into a loose tribal federation, which exerted control over the subject Phrygian peasants. During the early phase of their settlement, the Galatians mostly supported themselves by plundering bordering countries or by serving as mercenaries in the various Hellenistic armies of the time. In 232 BC, the Attalids of Pergamon finally defeated them in battle, and this eventually led to the creation of a more permanent Galatian settlement in central Anatolia that became a vassal of the Hellenistic Kingdom of Pergamon. In 189 BC, after having transformed the Kingdom of Pergamon into their province of Asia, the Romans launched a large expedition against the Celts of Anatolia that became known as the Galatian War. After being defeated, the Galatians lost much of their military power and were later invaded by Mithridates VI of Pontus. Thanks to the decisive help of the Romans, however, the Celts of Anatolia were later able to regain their independence after the end of the Mithridatic Wars (88–63 BC) that were fought between Pontus and the Roman Republic. In 62 BC, Galatia formally became a client state of Rome and was officially organized as a kingdom, but in 25 BC, this Kingdom of Galatia was finally annexed by the Romans. From 62 BC, Galatia deployed a regular army organized according to contemporary Roman models and trained by Roman military officers. Deiotarus, who was made King of Galatia in 62 BC as a reward for the military support given to Pompey, restructured the military forces of his realm into thirty *cohortes* (the equivalent of three Roman legions) and levied a total of 14,000 soldiers (12,000 infantry and 2,000 cavalry). These took part in the wars against Mithridathes of Pontus as loyal allies of Rome, but after suffering several heavy defeats they had to be reduced to a single 'legion'. This unit, however, continued to fight on the side of the Romans during Caesar's brief campaign against Pontus in 47 BC. After the death of Caesar, the Galatians made a crucial mistake: they decided to side with Mark Antony and thus lost their independence after he was defeated in 30 BC. With Galatia's incorporation into the Roman Empire, the single 'legion' of the kingdom was absorbed into the Roman Army as the Legio XXII Deiotariana (from the name of the king who had founded it).

Roman *Aquilifer* carrying the small round shield that was typical of standard-bearers. (*Photo by Marc Seriol [@marcmarkhus_photo] and copyright by Legio II Traiana Fortis – Cohors I Barcinonum, Barcino Oriens*)

Rear view of a Roman *Aquilifer*. All the standard-bearers of the legion wore an animal skin over their head and shoulders. (*Photo by Marc Seriol [@marcmarkhus_photo] and copyright by Legio II Traiana Fortis – Cohors I Barcinonum, Barcino Oriens*)

Chapter 5

The Conquest of Britannia

In Britain, the Iron Age began around 600 BC, about a century before it did in Ireland, and it was during this period that the Celtic influence became increasingly strong in the British Isles. The 'Celticization' of Britain was not characterized by mass migrations or by violent campaigns of conquest. Although a good number of Celts arrived in Britain from northern Gaul, these settled on British territory in a peaceful way and soon integrated with the local populations (who were already organized in tribes). Over time, especially during the fourth century BC, the whole population of Britain assumed the main characteristics of the Celtic La Tène culture: the presence of the early immigrants from Gaul had been fundamental in this sense, with a quite limited number of settlers having been able to influence and change forever the civilization of the British Isles' original inhabitants. This process happened a little more slowly in Ireland, Scotland and Wales, but had more permanent results than in Britain. By the end of the fourth century BC, the whole British Isles had become the home of hundreds of Celtic tribes: only Gaul could be considered as more 'Celticized' than Britain. After his early victories over the Celts of Gaul, Caesar turned his attention to the Britons in order to punish them for their recent support given to the Celts of Armorica (modern Brittany). The Romans disembarked in southern England with two legions, but Caesar's campaign was a failure due to bad weather destroying a large part of the Roman fleet and the landings being opposed very effectively by the Britons (who employed war chariots on a large scale, something that the Romans were not prepared to face). In 54 BC, Caesar returned to Britain at the head of a larger force and this time had made all the necessary preparations to face the Britons on equal terms. The Catuvellauni, the most important Celtic tribe in southern England, were defeated and obliged to pay a yearly tribute to Rome. Although Caesar's expeditions in Britain had not given new territories to Rome, they were extremely important for his propaganda as no other Roman military commander had ever ventured so far north (reaching what was known as the 'edge of the world').

Around AD 40, only the Celts of Britain and Ireland remained independent from Rome: thanks to their relative geographical isolation, they had been able to preserve their identity from the great political and cultural changes taking place in Europe at that time. Once the Roman Empire was consolidated in Continental Europe, the Romans could seriously start planning an invasion of Britain. Following Caesar's expeditions, the Celts of southern Britain had continued to send tributes and hostages to Rome in order to retain their independence. From the time of Augustus, however, it became clear that the Romans would occupy the island at the first opportunity. In AD 43, Claudius, the fourth emperor of Rome, finally ordered the invasion of Britain, which was conducted by an army of 40,000 men, half of whom were professional soldiers from four legions (II Augusta, IX Hispana, XIV Gemina and XX Valeria Victrix). From a political point of view, the Roman invasion of Britain was determined by Claudius' will to obtain control over the important natural resources of the island, that had already been noticed by Caesar; militarily, it was carried out to protect northern Gaul from possible Celtic incursions from the British Isles. The early resistance of the Britons was guided by the Catuvellauni, the powerful confederation of tribes that had already fought against Julius Caesar. The decisive battle of this first phase of the campaign was fought at the River Medway, where the Celts assembled an army to stop the Romans who had landed at Richborough, on the east coast of Kent. Upon hearing of the Roman landing, the Britons of south-eastern England assembled a very large force – probably numbering around 100,000 warriors – and put it under the orders of two warlords of the Catuvellauni, the brothers Togodumnus and Caratacus. The Britons had one objective: to stop the Roman advance by using the River Medway as a natural barrier. For the invaders, crossing the river in front of a large enemy force and under a rain of arrows and javelins would have been tactical suicide. No bridge crossed the Medway, and thus the Britons were confident of victory, but the Romans could count on a special military resource of which the Celtic leaders were ignorant – a large contingent of Germanic auxiliary cavalrymen, recruited from the Batavi tribe, who were specifically trained to cross rivers wearing their heavy chainmail. The Batavian cavalrymen rapidly crossed the Medway and launched a surprise attack against the Britons, engaging their war chariots. Taking advantage of the enemy's surprise, the Legio II Augusta also crossed the river under the command of Vespasian (a future Emperor). The Britons were unable to mount an effective counter-attack, and by the end of the first day of battle the whole Roman expeditionary force had crossed the Medway. During the following days, the Romans resumed their attacks, inflicting severe losses on the Britons, who resisted with great determination, but in the end they had to abandon their positions. Unlike the Celts of Gaul, those living in Britannia were lightly equipped and had never fought against a large heavy infantry force consisting of four legions. Consequently, their defeat on the Medway was almost inevitable.

After this first major battle, the Britons fell back to the Thames, where they soon organized a new line of defence. The Roman troops, however, moved very rapidly and attacked the Britons while some of their warriors were still crossing the river. The invaders were able to build a temporary bridge across the Thames, and thus the new Celtic defensive line was breached without a major battle being fought.

Detail of the helmet of a Roman Aquilifer, covered with the head of a wolf. (*Photo by Marc Seriol [@marcmarkhus_photo] and copyright by Legio II Traiana Fortis – Cohors I Barcinonum, Barcino Oriens*)

Roman *Cornicen* with *lorica segmentata*. (*Photo by Marc Seriol* [*@marcmarkhus_photo*] *and copyright by Legio II Traiana Fortis – Cohors I Barcinonum, Barcino Oriens*)

During the minor skirmishes that took place in the area of the Thames, the warlord Togodumnus died. This was a major blow for the Celtic communities, which were now in a very chaotic political situation. Several tribes, considering the recent defeats to be decisive, wanted to make peace with the Romans, whereas others wanted to continue fighting using guerrilla tactics in order to halt the advance of the invaders. At this point of the campaign, Emperor Claudius went to Britannia, having understood that it was on the verge of being conquered. A total of eleven tribes surrendered to Claudius without putting up further resistance. The Romans had occupied most of south-eastern England, but to the north and the west there were still several warlike communities with intact military capabilities.

The Romans established their capital at Camulodunum (modern Colchester in Essex), but Caratacus had evaded capture and was able to continue his resistance in the west after Claudius left Britannia to celebrate his triumph in Rome. Vespasian, the most brilliant Roman commander serving in Britain, took part of the invading forces and advanced westwards, where he subdued many tribes and conquered several enemy fortified camps, advancing as far as Exeter. The Legio IX Hispana, meanwhile, was sent north towards Lincoln with orders to subdue the local Celtic communities. By AD 47, after just one major battle and a handful of years of campaigning, the whole of present-day England had been conquered by Rome and transformed into a province. During that year, the new Roman governor of Britannia, Publius Ostorius Scapula, launched a first military campaign against the Celtic tribes of Wales. These tribesmen defended their homelands fiercely and caused several problems for the Romans. In AD 50, Roman troops finally intercepted Caratacus and his forces, obliging them to fight a pitched battle. This clash, known as the Battle of Caer Caradoc, ended with the defeat of the two tribes that supported the rebel leader: the Ordovices and the Silures. Caratacus' family was captured, but the warlord escaped once again, fleeing north, where the resistance of the Britons continued. Here, however, he was captured by the Brigantes, who were – temporarily – allies of Rome and who handed him over to the invaders in chains. Ostorius Scapula then died and was replaced as governor of Britannia by Aulus Didius Gallus, who – by using harsh methods – was able to subdue the warlike Celtic communities living on the border between England and Wales. The new governor, however, made little progress in extending the Roman presence westwards and northwards. In AD 54, following the death of Claudius, Nero became the new emperor. Being very ambitious and searching for military glory, the young monarch decided to enlarge the Roman possessions in Britain and thus appointed Quintus Veranius as the new governor. Veranius, an experienced administrator, was able to organize a successful campaign in Wales, which ended with the subjugation of most of the local tribes.

Quintus Veranius, understanding that the resistance of the Britons, especially in Wales, was guided by the druids, tried to kill as many of them as possible. In Celtic Britain, the druids were not only religious guides but also political leaders, who could assemble substantial numbers of warriors in case of war. In AD 60, the Romans destroyed an important druidical centre located on the island of Mona (modern Anglesey), which deprived the rebels of their leadership. Despite this, the final occupation of Wales could not be achieved due to the outbreak of a major rebellion in England. This is commonly known as 'Boudicca's Revolt', from the name of the queen of the Iceni who guided it. The Iceni were one of the most important Celtic tribes living in south-eastern Britain; they had already fought against Rome in AD 47, but had been soundly defeated. Despite this, the Romans permitted them to retain some degree of autonomy. With the ascendancy of Boudicca, the Iceni took advantage of the Romans' heavy military involvement in Wales to launch a general rebellion. Boudicca was in many ways the female equivalent of Vercingetorix: thanks to her great charisma, she was able to unite most of the Celtic tribes of Britannia against the Romans. The revolt clearly showed that the Roman presence in Britain was not yet well consolidated, since the druids were still the real masters of the territory. Most of the tribes had formally submitted to Rome only to gain time to reorganize their forces. Initially, Boudicca's rebel army was victorious in numerous encounters. The rebel Britons' first target was Camulodunum, which was inhabited by Roman veterans who had decided to settle in Britain after years of fighting. The colonists had badly mistreated the local Celts in many ways, for example by obliging them to pay for the construction of a temple that was built in honour of the former emperor, Claudius. The Roman veterans, realizing that the locals were on the verge of revolt, asked for help from the new governor of Britannia, Catus Decianus. The reinforcements the governor sent, however, consisted of just 200 auxiliaries, which was far too few to stop the Britons. Camulodunum was destroyed after bitter fighting, the last veterans resisting inside Claudius' temple for two days. In a bid to end the rebellion, the Legio IX Hispana marched against Boudicca, but was routed in battle and practically destroyed. The Britons took advantage of this victory to march on Londinium (present-day London), a new Roman settlement that was growing rapidly as a thriving commercial centre. Boudicca destroyed Londinium as she had already done with Camulodunum. At this point, the Britons seemed invincible and the Roman presence in Britannia appeared to be on the point of ending. The Romans, however, were able to mount a counter-offensive with all the forces at their disposal. A task force consisting of the Legio XIV Gemina, some detachments of the Legio XX Valeria Victrix and a large number of auxiliaries marched against Boudicca. The decisive clash of the war, known as the Battle of Watling Street, then took place, with 10,000 Romans facing around 100,000 Britons. Initially, the Romans did not move from their positions, throwing their heavy

Roman *Cornicen*. (*Photo by Marc Seriol* [*@marcmarkhus_photo*] *and copyright by Legio II Traiana Fortis – Cohors I Barcinonum, Barcino Oriens*)

Roman auxiliary infantryman with *lorica hamata* and oval shield. (*Photo by Marc Seriol [@marcmarkhus_photo] and copyright by Legio II Traiana Fortis – Cohors I Barcinonum, Barcino Oriens*)

javelins against the assaulting enemy formations and inflicting serious losses on them. The Romans then dashed forward in a wedge-like formation, while the auxiliary cavalry, deployed on the Roman wings, charged against the Britons, who were unable to stop the attack and soon took to flight. The escape of Boudicca's warriors from the battlefield was made more difficult by the fact that the Britons had deployed their wagons at the back of their formation. The Romans took advantage of this and gave no quarter to their defeated enemies, killing every man, woman or child they encountered in the Britons' rearguard. A total of 80,000 Celts – both warriors and civilians – were massacred in the viciously fought battle. Boudicca, seeing her forces decisively defeated and her revolt crushed, ended her life by taking poison.

From AD 61–70, the Romans completed their conquest of Wales and expanded their territories into northern Britain. In AD 78, the great military commander Gnaeus Julius Agricola arrived in Britain as the new Roman governor of the province. An experienced leader, Agricola's main objective was to expand Roman-held territory towards Scotland (known as Caledonia by the Romans). After defeating the last independent tribes of northern England, including the warlike Brigantes, he pushed his troops further north to the Firth of Tay without meeting any serious resistance. The advancing Romans built several forts in the newly conquered areas in order to secure their presence in northern England.

Ancient Scotland was inhabited by some of the wildest and most warlike Celtic tribes ever encountered by Rome. They had experienced very little contact with other civilizations in the past, and were much more difficult to conquer than the tribes of southern Britain. Thanks to an intelligent use of amphibious tactics, Agricola was able to move along Scotland's eastern and northern coasts, reaching the very heart of the eastern Highlands, where he finally met a large Caledonian army in the Battle of Mons Graupius. The exact location of this pivotal battle is still unknown, but it is known for sure that it was fought in northern Scotland. The Caledonian tribes had assembled a large army with 30,000 warriors, commanded by the warlord Calgacus. They faced Agricola's command of around 18,000 men (comprising both legionaries and auxiliaries). The Celts deployed their warriors on the high ground of Mons Graupius in a horseshoe formation. On the plain, in front of the Romans, there were numerous Caledonian war chariots. After a brief exchange of missile weapons, Agricola ordered his auxiliaries (most of whom were Germani) to launch a frontal attack against the enemy. The Caledonians were swiftly cut down by the Romans on the lower slopes of Mons Graupius. Outflanked by Agricola's cavalry, they were completely routed. The Romans launched a relentless pursuit, killing around 10,000 of their enemy. Before being recalled to Rome in AD 84, Agricola built a network of military roads and forts to secure Roman control over both the Highlands and the Lowlands.

Roman auxiliary infantryman. (*Photo and copyright by Legio XI C.P.F. Hispaniensis*)

After Agricola's departure, however, the succeeding Roman governors of Britain did little to consolidate the conquest of Caledonia and to protect the communication and supply lines connecting south-eastern Scotland with north-eastern England. The fortifications were abandoned and most of the local Celtic tribes were able to

Roman auxiliary infantryman with *lorica hamata*. (*Photo and copyright by David Burns of Legio XIIII Gemina*)

Roman auxiliary infantryman with *lorica hamata*. (*Photo and copyright by David Burns of Legio XIIII Gemina*)

Roman auxiliary infantryman. Note the protective leather cover of the oval shield. (*Photo and copyright by David Burns of Legio XIIII Gemina*)

Roman officer of the auxiliary infantry, with crested helmet and *manica*. (*Photo and copyright by David Burns of Legio XIIII Gemina*)

rapidly regain their previous autonomy. Gradually the Romans retreated back to the border between northern England and southern Scotland, where a stable *limes* was established from AD 122 thanks to the construction of Hadrian's Wall from the North Sea in the east to the Irish Sea in the west. During the following two decades, the Romans attempted to reoccupy the Scottish Lowlands, but encountered strong resistance from the Caledonians. Accepting that it was impossible to move further north against the Scottish Highlands, in AD 142 they established a new *limes* by building the Antonine Wall that separated the Lowlands from the Highlands. Despite these efforts, in AD 162, the Romans were forced to abandon the Lowlands and to retreat back to the stronger obstacle of Hadrian's Wall. During the following decades, the Romans made at least four significant attempts to reconquer southern Caledonia, but all these were repulsed.

Roman auxiliary light infantryman, with sun hat and *cingulum militiae* (the traditional Roman military belt). (*Photo by Marc Seriol [@arcmarkhus_photo] and copyright by Legio II Traiana Fortis – Cohors I Barcinonum, Barcino Oriens*)

Chapter 6

The Great Jewish Revolt and the Parthian Campaigns

Until AD 4, most of present-day Israel was ruled as a client kingdom of Rome by Herod the Great, who was a loyal ally of Mark Antony but later supported Augustus when he gained the upper hand in the final phase of Rome's civil wars. Herod was a tyrant, who killed every individual who could claim his throne, but he protected the integrity of his state from foreign aggressions and retained a certain degree of autonomy from Rome. After his death, the kingdom of Judea was divided into four parts between his three surviving sons and his sister, Salome I. This so-called Herodian Tetrarchy, however, did not last long as the Romans used their military presence in Syria to annex – one by one – the four small Jewish states to the expanding Empire. By AD 44, all the states of the Herodian Tetrarchy had disappeared and Judaea could be finally organized as a Roman territory (dependent on the adjacent province of Syria). Initially, the Romans respected the laws and customs of the Jewish people, for example by allowing their new subjects to rest on the Sabbath or by granting them exemption from pagan rituals. During the following decades, however, the situation started to change as the Romans tried to 'hellenize' the Jews by introducing the Greek language and pagan culture on a large scale in Israel. In AD 64, Gessius Florus became procurator of Judea, and his actions accelerated the ongoing escalation towards the outbreak of a major rebellion. Florus stole riches from the treasure of the sacred Temple of Jerusalem and executed many Jewish traditionalists who tried to defend their culture from Roman influence. What later became known as the Great Jewish Revolt began as a clash between opposing Jewish factions, with confrontations between those Jews who wanted to rebel against the Romans and those who favoured the occupation. Florus reacted to the unrest by sending his soldiers into Jerusalem and arresting some of the rebel leaders. The Jews were outraged by these actions and took up arms against the Roman garrisons stationed on their territory. Within a few days the legionaries were expelled from Jerusalem and from the fortress of Masada, the strongest fortification in Judea that had been built by Herod the Great.

Rome's military garrison of Judaea was not particularly strong, since it could count on the support of the legions that were stationed in nearby Syria. The governor of the latter province, Cestius Gallus, soon assembled an army of 30,000 men (including the

Roman auxiliary archer from the eastern provinces of the Empire. (*Photo by Marc Seriol* [*@marcmarkhus_photo*] *and copyright by Legio II Traiana Fortis – Cohors I Barcinonum, Barcino Oriens*)

Rear view of a Roman auxiliary archer from the eastern provinces of the Empire. Note the piece of scale armour applied on the back of the helmet for protection of the neck. (*Photo by Marc Seriol [@ arcmarkhus_photo] and copyright by Legio II Traiana Fortis – Cohors I Barcinonum, Barcino Oriens*)

Legio XII Fulminata, detachments from other legions and many auxiliaries) that was sent to reconquer Judea. Initially, the Romans obtained a series of victories and killed thousands of rebels; they even retook most of Jerusalem, but were unable to occupy the strongly fortified citadel. At this point, the Roman commanders, finding themselves surrounded by hostile groups of Jewish fighters, decided to abandon Jerusalem and move towards the sea to await reinforcements. During their march, however, the Romans were ambushed at the pass of Beth Horon by 25,000 Jewish insurgents. The Roman force, which comprised just 6,000 men, was completely outnumbered. The Jews attacked the Roman troops from a distance with stones and arrows, and the legionaries were massacred: they had not been able to get into formation due to the nature of the terrain and thus had lost their usual cohesion. After the Battle of Beth Horon, the Jewish rebels equipped themselves with many weapons taken from the bodies of dead Romans and enlarged their forces thanks to the arrival of many new volunteers. The shocking defeat convinced Emperor Nero to appoint Vespasian as commander of a large expeditionary corps that was assembled to reconquer Judea. His army comprised the Legio X Fretensis and Legio V Macedonica, which were later joined by the Legio XV Apollinaris from Egypt (which was commanded by Vespasian's son and future emperor, Titus). Meanwhile, the Jewish leaders formed a provisional government in Jerusalem and began reinforcing the defences of the city, expecting a massive Roman counter-offensive. Having around 60,000 soldiers under his command, Vespasian used the political and religious divisions existing among the Jews to his advantage. Consequently, he reconquered most of Galilee in northern Israel during AD 67 without meeting any serious resistance.

Vespasian made the important coastal city of Caesarea Marittima his main base, from where he methodically proceeded to cleanse the Judean coastline of insurgent groups. During this phase of the war, more than 100,000 Jews were killed or sold into slavery. The Jewish defenders of Jerusalem then started to experience a series of internal conflicts: the radical faction of the Zealots was determined to defend the city until the last man, while other groups wanted to avoid the destruction of their holy capital. In the end, after thousands of moderate Jews were killed, the Zealots gained the upper hand and obtained full control over Jerusalem. The first half of AD 69 saw the Romans reconquering most of Judea at a time when the very heart of the Empire was shattered by a bloody civil war which saw the ascendancy and fall of three emperors, but this did not affect the military operations taking place in Judea. Eventually, Vespasian was acclaimed as emperor by the legions under his command. As a result, having decided to end the civil war by assuming the imperial title for himself, he went to Rome and left his son, Titus, to finish the war against the Jews. Titus advanced through the hill country surrounding Jerusalem with great determination, killing

Roman auxiliary archer with bronze helmet. (*Photo and copyright by Legio XI C.P.F. Hispaniensis*)

Roman auxiliary slinger from the Balearic Islands. (*Photo by Marc Seriol [@ arcmarkhus_photo] and copyright by Legio II Traiana Fortis – Cohors I Barcinonum, Barcino Oriens*)

Roman auxiliary slinger from the Balearic Islands. (*Photo by Marc Seriol [@marcmarkhus_photo] and copyright by Legio II Traiana Fortis – Cohors I Barcinonum, Barcino Oriens*)

anyone who tried to stop his march, leading to an immense wave of Jewish refugees fleeing to the capital in search of shelter. The Romans surrounded Jerusalem and initiated a lengthy siege, which proved particularly difficult for them. The legionaries were unable to breach Jerusalem's strong defences, and were forced to dig a trench around the circumference of the city walls and build an external wall that was as high as those of the capital. Having constructed massive ramparts, the legionaries were finally able to assault the enemy positions. The resistance of the Jews was desperate, with almost all the civilians trapped inside the city taking up arms against the Romans. In the summer of AD 70, after a siege lasting seven months, Titus took advantage of the collapse of some sections of Jerusalem's walls to enter the city and burn it to the ground. The Temple, one of the last bastions defended by the Zealots, was completely destroyed like all the other buildings. Thousands of captured Jews became slaves and the Temple's treasures, including the Menorah (the golden candelabra of Moses) and the Table of the Bread of God's Presence, were transported to Rome in order to be paraded during the triumph of Titus. The fall of Jerusalem, however, did not mark the end of the Great Jewish Revolt, which continued until AD 73 when all the remaining rebel strongholds were taken by the Romans (including the strongest one of Masada, which fell only after an epic siege that ended with the suicide of all the remaining Jewish defenders). During the following decades, Judea rose up in revolt on several occasions, most notably during AD 115–117 and later from AD 132–136. The Romans, however, were always able to crush the national revolts of the Jews. From AD 136 onwards, thousands of Jews left Judea for other areas of the Mediterranean, thereby initiating the long and complex historical process known as the Jewish Diaspora.

Lead projectiles and leather bag used by the Balearic slingers in Roman service. The inscriptions on the projectiles had an apotropaic function. (*Photo by Marc Seriol [@marcmarkhus_photo] and copyright by Legio II Traiana Fortis – Cohors I Barcinonum, Barcino Oriens*)

The most implacable enemy of the Romans in the Middle East was the Parthian Empire, a major military Asian power that had combat capabilities comparable to those of the Roman Empire. The Parthians, originally a nomadic people living in north-eastern Iran, had gradually been able to create an empire in the Middle East under the guidance of their ambitious Arsacid dynasty. By taking advantage of the Seleucid Empire's great internal and external difficulties, they had conquered the whole territory of Iran and had later reached the borders of Syria (the heartland of the Seleucids) after having securely established themselves in Iraq. The Parthian armies consisted entirely of cavalry: mounted archers armed with deadly composite bows and heavy cavalrymen covered with armour. The Seleucids were defeated on several occasions by this combination of light and heavy cavalry, which proved extremely effective tactically. The Parthians knew how to fight for long periods in desert areas and had an excellent logistical organization, while their archers were superb skirmishers, who could fire their arrows with great accuracy, even when their horses were running away from their target (this being known as the famous 'Parthian shot', from which we have 'parting shot'). The Parthian heavy cavalrymen, or cataphracts, were equipped with long spears and rode armoured horses. When charging at full gallop, their power was impressive.

When the Seleucid Empire crumbled, the Romans occupied Syria and its other western regions, while the Parthians took control of Iraq and other eastern areas. It quickly became apparent, however, that the two emerging powers of the Middle East would have to fight each other for dominance of the whole region: the Romans wanted Iraq, while the Parthians had eyes on Syria. The first major Roman-Parthian conflict took place in 53 BC and ended with a disastrous defeat for the Roman Republic, a large Roman army commanded by Crassus being completely wiped out at the Battle of Carrhae. The Romans were defeated because they had underestimated the military capabilities of the Parthians. During the Roman civil wars of the following years, the Parthians first sided with Pompey against Caesar and then with Brutus and Cassius (the murderers of Caesar) against Mark Antony and Octavianus Augustus. In 36 BC, Mark Antony led an inconclusive military campaign against the Parthians, which failed to achieve any decisive result for Rome. After becoming princeps, Augustus tried to solve the 'Parthian problem' through diplomacy, since he had no intention of fighting a new war against the Arsacids. He obtained the restitution of several Roman standards that had been captured by the Parthians at Carrhae and transformed Armenia into a client kingdom of the Roman Empire. Because of its geographical position, isolated between Parthian north-western Iran and Roman Anatolia, Armenia soon became extremely important for Rome because it acted as a buffer zone between the two rival empires. In AD 58, following many years of increasing tensions, a new conflict broke out between

Roman auxiliary cavalryman armed with spear and javelins. (*Photo and copyright by David Burns of Legio XIIII Gemina*)

Rear view of a Roman auxiliary cavalryman equipped with oval shield. (*Photo and copyright by David Burns of Legio XIIII Gemina*)

the Romans and Parthians. The war began as a Roman military intervention in an ongoing Armenian civil conflict, which saw the clash of a weak pro-Roman faction against a strong pro-Parthian faction. Roman forces, including three legions (the III Gallica, IV Scythica and VI Ferrata), initially obtained a series of easy successes and were able to occupy the two capitals of Armenia: Artaxata and Tigranocerta. In AD 61, the Parthians mounted a massive counter-offensive with substantial numbers of troops. They attempted to besiege Tigranocerta, without success, but later surrounded a large Roman force at the Battle of Rhandeia and obliged it to surrender. In AD 63, hostilities came to an end with a compromise: the pretender supported by the Parthians obtained the Armenian throne, but he had to swear loyalty towards Rome as a vassal king of the Empire.

During the following decades, both the Romans and Parthians continued to plot in Armenia in order to augment their political influence in the kingdom. In AD 113, however, Emperor Trajan – who had already conquered Dacia and had laid claim to be the greatest military leader in the history of the Empire – decided to launch a large-scale invasion to conquer Parthia. The *casus belli* for the conflict was that the Parthians had installed a new monarch on the Armenian throne who was very much favourable to them, but it soon became clear that the war would be a struggle to the death for both empires. Trajan, as he had always done beforehand, planned the campaign in minute detail and assembled a large invasion force comprising a total of ten legions. He first invaded Armenia, deposing the pro-Parthian king and annexing the realm to the Roman Empire as a new province. He then marched towards the Taurus Mountains to occupy the area of northern Mesopotamia (modern Iraq) located between the Tigris and Euphrates rivers. The Parthians were unable to stop the invaders and had to abandon several major Mesopotamian cities. After spending the winter of AD 115/116 in Antioch, Trajan resumed his offensive and divided his forces into two columns: the first crossed the Tigris and then moved towards southern Mesopotamia, while the second captured the city of Babylon. Having come to the narrow strip of land located between the Euphrates and the Tigris, Trajan reunited his armies and marched on the ancient Seleucid capital of Seleucia. Without having to fight a single major pitched battle, he also entered the Parthian capital of Ctesiphon. The Parthians had been completely taken by surprise by the strategic intelligence and logistical mastery of Trajan's Romans, who supplied their advancing troops throughout the campaign and transported a fleet of warships on the Tigris and Euphrates. Trajan then reached the Persian Gulf and occupied the territory of modern Kuwait.

For the first time in their history, the Romans reached the Indian Ocean and were able to organize Mesopotamia as a province: the Roman Empire had reached its maximum territorial extent and had decisively defeated the Parthians. The Roman success, however, did not last long, since the newly conquered territories proved too vast to be properly garrisoned and were inhabited by peoples hostile to Rome. As soon as Trajan left the Persian Gulf for Babylon, the Parthians launched a counter-offensive against Mesopotamia and Armenia from Iran. The Romans responded by reinforcing their positions in northern Mesopotamia, but were forced to abandon southern Mesopotamia. During this final phase of the war, Trajan's health started to fail him, and the emperor died during the siege of the enemy fortified city of Hatra, probably after suffering heat stroke. With Trajan's death in AD 117, the war between the Romans and Parthians soon came to an end. The new emperor, Hadrian, promptly reversed his predecessor's policy of expansion in the Middle East. He decided that the Euphrates would mark the border between Roman and Parthian territory, and consequently the *status quo* of the region was restored and Mesopotamia was returned to the Parthians. Armenia remained a vassal kingdom of the Roman Empire, albeit enjoying a greater degree of autonomy than previously.

War over Armenia broke out again between the Roman and Parthian empires in AD 161, when a Parthian army defeated the Roman forces in Armenia and ravaged part of Roman Syria. The Romans responded by organizing an effective counter-attack, which ended with the defeat of the Parthians in Armenia and the installation of a new, pro-Roman monarch on the country's throne. After having taken the initiative, the Romans launched a new invasion of Mesopotamia in AD 164 with the objective of reconquering the territories that had once been occupied by Trajan. They won two battles against the Parthians (at Dura-Europos and Seleucia) and were able to sack the Parthian capital of Ctesiphon in AD 165. Nevertheless, the outbreak of an epidemic, possibly of smallpox, ended the war just when it seemed that the Romans were on the verge of victory. The *status quo* of the Middle East was again restored, but the legionaries who had participated in the conflict brought the epidemic to other territories of the Empire, initiating what became known as the Antonine Plague. Throughout the long history of the Empire, the Romans were never able to eliminate the Parthian presence in the Middle East. Emperor Septimius Severus invaded Mesopotamia again between AD 195 and 197, while Emperor Caracalla also attacked the Parthians in AD 216 and 217, but neither of these conflicts were decisive and the balance of power in the region remained largely unchanged. The Parthian Empire was finally destroyed only in AD 226, when a new Persian dynasty – that of the Sassanids – emerged in Iran and conquered the city of Ctesiphon after a brief but bloody conflict. The Sassanids established a centralized state that was militarily much stronger than the semi-nomadic Parthian one, which enabled them to invade Roman territory on several occasions during the later centuries of the Empire.

Roman legionary cavalryman with bronze helmet. (*Photo and copyright by Legio XI C.P.F. Hispaniensis*)

Roman legionary cavalryman with hexagonal shield. (*Photo and copyright by Legio XI C.P.F. Hispaniensis*)

Chapter 7

The Year of the Four Emperors

During the period taken into account in this book, the Roman Empire endured a single major civil war that took place during the crucial year of AD 69, which saw the end of the Julio-Claudian dynasty that had been created by Augustus and the ascendancy of the new Flavian dynasty founded by Vespasian. Since the beginning of the principate, the Roman emperors had always experienced numerous problems relating to their succession. The imperial monarchy of Rome was not established according to hereditary principles like other states around the Mediterranean. Starting from Augustus, the emperors usually adopted an heir who was part of their family but was not their son; in most cases, in fact, ruling emperors did not have direct heirs. The system based on the adoption principle worked well for some of the early emperors, but soon began to show its limits. Since no official dynasty existed, both the Senate and the Praetorian Guard could influence the election of new monarchs by using their political or military influence. Court intrigues taking place in Rome started to determine the leadership of the Empire, a situation that was not welcomed by the Roman elites living in the provinces or the superior military officers commanding the legions in the field; indeed, these men wanted to play their own important role in the political processes that led to the appointment of the new emperors. Over time, the will of the legionaries became the most important factor behind the election of new emperors, since most of Rome's power came via the weapons of the legions. Since the Empire was still going through an expansionist phase of its history, it needed a strong military leadership to continue flourishing. The legions fully understood this situation, and thus always supported potential emperors who had extensive military experience. Very often, the will of the legionaries ran counter to that of the elite Praetorians, who were highly corrupted and usually supported candidates who promised them large sums of money. The Senate, meanwhile, was favourable (on most occasions) to potential emperors who came from the aristocratic families of Rome and who wanted to limit the powers of the emperor.

The contrasting interests described above became apparent when the Julio-Claudian dynasty came to an end with the death of Nero. He had governed Rome well during the first years of his rule, but later made a series of terrible mistakes. He proved himself unable to deal with the complex defence of the imperial lands, increased taxation above all limits, persecuted the members of the Senate who tried to limit his personal powers, wasted enormous sums of money on futile ventures, failed to crush the Great Jewish Revolt and was even believed to have caused the Great Fire of Rome in AD 64. Sensing that Nero would soon destroy the Empire due to his personal ambition and mental problems, the members of the Senate started to conspire against him. An initial plot, known as the Pisonian Conspiracy, attempted to remove Nero and to restore the Republic in AD 65, but was discovered by the emperor (who ordered the execution of many important personalities, including Seneca). Then in AD 68, the governor of Gallia Lugdunensis, Gaius Julius Vindex, rebelled against Nero's tax policy and started planning to replace the emperor with Servius Sulpicius Galba (the experienced governor of Hispania Tarraconensis). Vindex's revolt, however, soon failed because the legions stationed on the Germanic border – the most powerful military formations in the Roman Empire – remained loyal to Nero and marched against Gallia Lugdunensis. In the early summer of AD 68, the commander of the Praetorian Guard, Nymphidius Sabinus, started to plot against the emperor and incited his men to transfer their loyalty from Nero to Galba. The Senate tried the emperor and condemned him to death as a 'public enemy' but Nero, abandoned by all his remaining supporters, committed suicide before he could be executed. With Nero's death, the Julio-Claudian dynasty came to an end and a period of complete anarchy began for the Roman Empire. Galba was invited to come to Rome as the new emperor at the head of a single legion (the VII Gemina), and was welcomed by the Senate. He was a moderate but capable administrator, who had served the Empire for most of his life. He respected the traditional prerogatives of the Senate and was determined to put an end to the abuses and the corruption that had been favoured by Nero during the later stages of his reign.

With Nero's death, the legions serving on the Germanic *limes* lost the possibility of receiving a generous reward of money for having crushed the rebellion of Vindex in Gaul. As a result, they did not accept Galba's rise to power. To prevent the outbreak of a military revolt on the Germanic border, Galba appointed Aulus Vitellius as the new commander of the legions, but it soon became clear that Vitellius was determined to use his new position only to increase his personal power and not to support the ruling emperor. Once in Rome, Galba cancelled all the laws that had been established by Nero and refused to pay the Praetorians the reward that had been promised to them by their commander, Nymphidius. At the beginning of AD 69, the legions in Germania refused to swear allegiance and obedience to Galba, the soldiers instead acclaiming their commander Vitellius as the new emperor. Upon hearing the news from the north, Galba decided to adopt a young senator, Lucius Calpurnius Piso Licinianus, as his successor in the hope of retaining the support of the Senate. His choice for the succession, however, offended the most influential and ambitious aristocrat of

Roman legionary cavalryman with oval shield. (*Photo and copyright by Legio XI C.P.F. Hispaniensis*)

Roman auxiliary cavalryman with parade helmet and shield. (*Photo and copyright by Robert Vermaat/ Ala I Batavorum*)

Rome, Marcus Salvius Otho, who had hoped to be Galba's successor himself. Otho bribed the Praetorian Guard and organized a military coup, and both Galba and Lucius were killed in the streets of Rome, together with their few supporters. At this point there were two emperors ruling at the same time: Otho, who was supported by

Rear view of a Roman auxiliary cavalryman armed with spear and javelins. (*Photo and copyright by Robert Vermaat/Ala I Batavorum*)

Roman auxiliary cavalryman with scale armour. (*Photo and copyright by Robert Vermaat/Ala I Batavorum*)

the Senate and the Praetorian Guard in Rome, and Vitellius, who had the backing of the legions in Germania. Hostilities between the two monarchs soon became unavoidable, since neither one had the intention of stepping down. Vitellius was backed by some of the finest legions of the Roman Army, which consisted of battle-hardened veterans of the Germanic Wars. These troops marched into Italy and, after obtaining several minor victories, finally met with Otho's forces at the First Battle of Bedriacum. The invading army of Vitellius included the Legio V Alaudae, Legio XXI Rapax and several vexillations (detachments) from other legions, in addition to a strong contingent of Batavian auxiliaries. Otho's forces comprised the Legio I Adiutrix, Legio XIII Gemina, Praetorian Guard and even a force of gladiators. The resulting battle was particularly violent, ending with a decisive victory for Vitellius, whose veterans proved they were soldiers of excellent quality. Following the clash, what remained of Otho's army surrendered and took an oath of allegiance to Vitellius. Otho chose to commit suicide rather than continuing a hopeless resistance. He had been emperor for fewer than three months, and had been the second Roman monarch – after Nero – to commit suicide. After making a triumphal entry into Rome, Vitellius was recognized as the new and legitimate emperor by the Senate.

Vitellius spent his days in Rome organizing banquets and triumphal parades, which had enormous costs for an imperial treasury that was already on the verge of bankruptcy. The emperor also began to act like a tyrant, ordering the torture and execution of all citizens who were suspected of being against him. While Vitellius consolidated his power in the capital of the Empire, the legions fighting in Judaea to crush the Great Jewish Revolt acclaimed their commander, Vespasian, as the new emperor. After having obtained the support of the governors of Egypt and Syria, Vespasian organized an expeditionary corps with the intention of invading Italy and removing Vitellius from the throne. Before his troops could reach the heart of the Empire, however, the legions stationed in the Danubian provinces of Raetia and Moesia also decided to rise up in revolt against Vitellius. They quickly marched on Italy after acclaiming Vespasian as emperor, and fought against the supporters of Vitellius in what became known as the Second Battle of Bedriacum. The army supporting Vespasian comprised the Legio III Gallica, Legio VII Claudia, Legio VIII Augusta, Legio VII Galbiana and Legio XIII Gemina, while the forces supporting Vitellius incorporated the Legio I Italica, Legio IV Macedonica, Legio V Alaudae, Legio XXI Rapax and Legio XXII Primigenia. The Second Battle of Bedriacum was a disaster for Vitellius, whose army was resoundingly defeated. He was captured in Rome when Vespasian's forces occupied the city, and was executed shortly afterwards. The dramatic 'Year of the Four Emperors' thus ended with the ascendancy to the throne of Vespasian and the creation of the new Flavian dynasty, which would rule Rome until AD 96.

Chapter 8

The Roman Conquest of Dacia

Around AD 70, the Dacian king Scorilo died and was succeeded by Duras, an ambitious warlord who was determined to continue the anti-Roman policy of his predecessor. Duras started to rebuild the military power of the Dacians and endeavoured to unify the various tribes of his people once again. In AD 85, Duras assembled a large army and invaded the Roman province of Moesia from the north. The attack met with great success, with the Romans proving unable to stop the Dacians. An entire legion was annihilated by the invaders, and the governor of Moesia, Oppius Sabinus, was killed during the major battle of the campaign. It became clear in Rome that something had changed in Dacia, and that there was now a strong enemy leader in that sector of the Danubian frontier who had the necessary military resources to occupy Moesia. Emperor Domitian, second son of Vespasian and last monarch of the Flavian dynasty, acted swiftly to counter Duras' offensive, going to Moesia at the head of a large military force and moved three legions to the territory of the threatened province. When the Roman troops arrived, however, the Dacians avoided a direct confrontation with the superior forces of Domitian. The war continued for several months, but without any major change in the strategic situation. On one occasion the Romans were ambushed and defeated by the Dacians, but they too also suffered some defeats. In AD 86/87, Duras decided to abdicate in favour of a younger Dacian war leader, Decebalus, who had been the main commander of the Dacians since the beginning of the conflict with Rome and had shown his great personal capabilities on several occasions. The new king soon understood that there was no point in continuing the war with Rome, at least for the time being, since the Roman garrison of Moesia was by now too strong to be defeated. As a result, after Emperor Domitian had already left the theatre of operations, a peace treaty was concluded between the Dacians and Romans. Under its terms, Decebalus returned the many Roman prisoners who had been captured by the Dacians and promised not to attack Moesia in the future. In exchange, he obtained Roman military assistance to build new fortifications on the territory of his kingdom and an annual subsidy of 8 million sesterces.

Thanks to these new fortifications that were built with the help of the Romans, Decebalus could complete the reunification of Dacia that had been initiated by his predecessor and transform it into a centralized state. With the large amounts of money sent every year by the Romans, he could also enlarge and re-equip his military forces (transforming them in a very efficient combat machine). Decebalus soon proved to be an excellent king, not only from a military point of view but also from an economic and administrative one. He started to exploit in a methodical way all the great mineral resources of his kingdom in order to produce larger amounts of precious metals, and also reorganized the structure of his state in order to exert better control over the peripheral areas of Dacia (where the local tribes were all brought under his influence). Furthermore, Decebalus ordered the creation of a fortified capital for his realm, which was known as Sarmizegetusa. Erected on top of a mountain, at an altitude of 1,200 metres, in the centre of the Dacian Kingdom, it soon became the most important political and religious location in Dacia. Sarmizegetusa, thanks to its position and fortifications, was extremely easy to defend; it comprised six connected citadels and was part of a larger system of fortifications. The site of Sarmizegetusa had already functioned as the capital of the Dacians during the reign of Burebista, but after his death it had lost its special status. In addition, before the rise of Decebalus, it had never been fortified or enlarged. During the decade that followed the end of hostilities between Dacia and Rome, Decebalus transformed his kingdom into one of the most flourishing states of Antiquity. He controlled a large portion of European territory, corresponding to modern Romania, and could field an impressive army of over 200,000 warriors. The Romans soon realized that signing a peace treaty with the Dacians had been a mistake, especially due to the lenient conditions offered to Decebalus. Sooner or later, Rome believed the Dacians would attack Moesia again, and thus the Empire had to be ready to react.

The Romans had bad memories of their previous war against the Dacians: the defeat of Oppius Sabinus and the humiliation suffered by the legions had not been forgotten. Decebalus had been the man responsible for that Roman setback, when he was still just a military commander and was known as Diurpaneus. He received the new name of Decebalus (meaning 'the Brave') only after defeating and killing Oppius Sabinus. In AD 97, Trajan became emperor of Rome and started to deal with the most important military issues of his state. He considered Dacia to be a substantial threat to the stability of the Empire, since it was too large to be considered a normal client state of Rome. In AD 101, after obtaining the Senate's official blessing, Trajan started his preparations for the invasion of Dacia. By conquering Dacia, the Romans would stabilize once and for all the northern borders of the Empire on the Danube. In addition, they would obtain access to the vast natural resources of a region that had never been fully explored. From a cultural point of view, Dacia was a kingdom located on the edges of the known world: the Romans had little knowledge

Roman auxiliary cavalryman wearing parade helmet with facial mask. (*Photo and copyright by Robert Vermaat/Ala I Batavorum*)

Roman auxiliary cavalryman. Note the rich parade harness worn by the horse. (*Photo and copyright by Robert Vermaat/Ala I Batavorum*)

of it and considered the Dacians to be one of the many barbarian peoples living on their frontiers. Nonetheless, Trajan prepared his invasion with great attention and assembled a large army to conduct it. The Dacians also made their preparations, under the intelligent guidance of Decebalus. In particular, the king made great efforts to conclude a military alliance with the Sarmatians. The latter were a nomadic people from the steppes of Central Asia, who had gradually driven out the Scythians from the plains of southern Russia and Ukraine during the third century BC. Like their Scythian enemies, the Sarmatians spent most of their life on horseback, their armies being made up of mounted archers equipped with composite bows and of cataphracts (cavalry with full armour) armed with heavy spears. As the years went by, the Sarmatians started to move south and practically eliminated the Scythians, occupying all their territories and establishing themselves north of Dacia. Decebalus was able to conclude a strong alliance with these steppe warriors, and in particular with the powerful tribe of the Roxolani, who provided him with large contingents of top-quality cavalry.

Trajan reached the Roman province of Moesia in the spring of AD 101 at the head of one of the largest forces ever assembled in the long history of Rome, which included fifteen legions, ten *vexillationes* of legions and eighty-nine corps of auxiliaries. The legions under his command were the I Adiutrix, I Italica, I Minervia, II Adiutrix, II Traiana Fortis, III Flavia, V Macedonica, VII Claudia, X Gemina, XI Claudia Pia Fidelis, XIII Gemina, XIV Gemina Martia Victrix, XV Apollinaris, XXI Rapax and XXX Ulpia Victrix. The vexillations came from the following legions: the II Augusta, III Augusta, III Gallica, IV Scythica, VI Ferrata, VII Gemina, IX Hispana, XII Fulminata, XX Valeria Victrix and XXII Primigenia. The corps of *auxilia* comprised twenty-one *alae* of cavalry, thirty-three *cohortes equitatae* (mixed infantry and cavalry), twenty-five *cohortes peditatae* (infantry) and ten *cohortes sagittariae* (archers). In total, Trajan could count on 75,000 legionaries and 55,000 auxiliaries, who were supplemented by another 20,000 *auxilia* soldiers transferred to Moesia specifically for this campaign (the other 55,000 auxilliaries were already stationed along the Danube before the outbreak of hostilities). The emperor also brought with him the Praetorian Guard. The Roman invasion force was divided into two large columns, which crossed the Danube on two pontoon bridges that were built with the ships of the Roman river fleet. Trajan's war plan was simple: he wanted to cross southern Dacia as soon as possible, ravaging all the enemy settlements encountered along the way, in order to reach the 'Iron Gates' very rapidly. These were a narrow mountain pass located west of the Dacian capital; capturing them was the only way to approach Sarmizegetusa and enter inside the main fortified system of the Dacians. During the first phase of the campaign, Decebalus acted very intelligently, avoiding any direct confrontation with the Romans and employing scorched earth tactics. All the food reserves in southern Dacia were moved north or destroyed before the Romans could capture them as the Dacians retreated towards the heart of their territories, obliging the Roman Army to move across densely forested areas.

The Romans knew very little about the interior regions of Dacia and thus, the further they advanced, the more stretched their supply lines became, to the point of being dangerously exposed to Dacian incursions. Trajan continued his advance very slowly and methodically, in order to avoid possible ambushes and to consolidate his presence in Dacian territory. While moving north, the Romans built camps, roads and bridges, infrastructure which would have helped them put up strong resistance in southern Dacia in case of defeat. Only when the Romans reached the Iron Gates did Decebalus decide that the time had come to fight a major pitched battle. This clash, which became known as the Second Battle of Tapae, was extremely hard-fought on both sides. The Romans were eventually able to repulse the Dacian assaults, but only after suffering severe losses. Decebalus also lost many warriors, but he had the time and resources to replace them. At this point of the campaign, the Dacians retreated behind the Iron Gates and inside their main fortified system, while the Romans built a massive winter camp not far from the entrance to the mountain pass. During the opening months of AD 102, with the Roman Army blocked outside the Iron Gates, Decebalus decided to strike on another front to divert Trajan's attention. Together with his Roxolani allies, he attacked Moesia from the north at the head of a massive military force. The Roman garrison of Moesia had great difficulties in containing Decebalus' invasion, but with the arrival of substantial reinforcements sent by Trajan the situation was stabilized. The Dacians and Roxolani made the fatal mistake of separating their forces, which enabled the Romans to react more effectively. Both the Dacians and Roxolani were thus defeated, obliging Decebalus to abandon his plans for the opening of a second front. Trajan then resumed his offensive in Dacia after having reorganized his army into three separate columns. These were to attack the Dacian fortifications from three different directions, having as their ultimate objective the conquest of Decebalus' capital.

The Romans, albeit with great difficulty, were able to capture several Dacian fortifications and started to encircle Sarmizegetusa. At this point, most likely in order to gain time and reorganize his defences, Decebalus sent emissaries to Trajan with offers of peace. The Romans responded by proposing very harsh conditions, which could not be accepted by Decebalus. Consequently, military operations soon resumed. During the following weeks, the Romans besieged and conquered all the Dacian fortifications located around Sarmizegetusa. The Dacians attacked the Roman troops while they were besieging the last stronghold, but were repulsed with

Roman legionary cavalryman with parade helmet and armour. Spears and javelins with painted shafts were used only on parade or during the *hippika gymnasia* (cavalry tournaments). (*Photo and copyright by Legio XI C.P.F. Hispaniensis*)

heavy losses. The way to the Dacian capital was now open for the Romans. Decebalus' army had been defeated in the field and there were no fortifications left in Dacian hands. The Romans, however, were extremely tired: they had suffered significant losses since the beginning of the war, and were by now far from their provinces. Trajan knew that a siege of Sarmizegetusa would have lasted for months, since the city was heavily fortified and built on top of a mountain, and that he could not sustain a new campaign in a hostile land, especially without proper supplies and fresh reinforcements. As a result, he decided to terminate hostilities and to conclude a peace treaty with Decebalus. The conditions imposed by the Romans were very harsh on the Dacians: Decebalus had to accept the presence of several Roman garrisons on his territory and was forced to give up all the weapons of his army. In addition, he

Roman auxiliary cavalryman with oval shield. (*Photo and copyright by Robert Vermaat/ Ala I Batavorum*)

Detail of a cavalry parade helmet with facial mask. (*Photo and copyright by Robert Vermaat/Ala I Batavorum*)

Detail of the decorated chanfron worn by Roman military horses during parades and tournaments. (*Photo and copyright by Robert Vermaat/Ala I Batavorum*)

was asked to destroy all the fortifications in his realm and to cede part of his southern territories to the Roman Empire. Finally, the Dacians were required to accept Rome's protection and thereby transform their kingdom into a client state of the Empire. Decebalus had no choice but to accept these humiliating conditions in order to gain time and prepare for a fresh war against Rome. In AD 102, military operations finally came to an end, at least for the moment. Soon after Trajan abandoned the theatre of operations with most of his troops, Decebalus started organizing himself for a new conflict. He re-equipped his whole army with new weapons and rebuilt the fortifications located around his capital that had been destroyed by the Romans. He attacked the Iazyges, a Sarmatian tribe that was allied with Rome, and ordered the execution of all those Dacian nobles who were in favour of respecting the peace treaty signed with the Romans.

Trajan responded to these events in AD 105 by moving towards Moesia again at the head of his forces. When the Romans arrived at the Danube, Trajan learned that his garrisons in Dacia had been massacred and that Decebalus was already waiting for him north of the river. Many Roman fortresses along the Danubian *limes* had been attacked and occupied by the Dacians, so Trajan had to spend the entire summer of AD 105 retaking these positions. In this early phase of the campaign, the Romans acknowledged that it had been a mistake not to besiege Sarmizegetusa during the previous conflict: it was clear to them that the only way to secure the Danubian frontier was to defeat Dacia and annex it to the Empire. Decebalus was too intelligent and ambitious to be a vassal king, so it was essential to conclude the war with his capture or execution. Understanding that conquering the whole of the Dacian Kingdom would be incredibly difficult, Trajan remained south of the Danube until AD 106, reorganizing the defences of Moesia and assembling more troops for the upcoming invasion. During these crucial months of preparation, the Romans also completed the construction of a permanent bridge across the Danube, thanks to which the Roman Army could move north at any time and receive supplies and reinforcements much more easily than in the previous clash with Decebalus. The Dacians were impressed by the building of this bridge, which was incredible for the standards of the time, but could do little to destroy it since it was defended by a substantial number of Roman troops. When it became clear that Trajan could cross the Danube at the head of a massive invasion force, the main allies of Decebalus decided to abandon the Dacians to their fate: the Roxolani and the Bastarnae, who had made up a considerable portion of Decebalus' armies during the previous conflict, proclaimed their neutrality in an attempt to avoid the bloody vengeance of the Romans.

While these events took place north of the Danube, Trajan strove to receive military support from the Iazyges and the Germanic tribes that were settled on Dacia's north-western border. He wanted to be sure that these peoples would not collaborate with

Decebalus, and even hoped that they could launch attacks from other directions and open further fronts against the Dacians. Once they saw that Decebalus had been abandoned by his allies, the Romans launched their invasion of Dacia. The Roman forces were divided into two large columns: one was to attack the fortifications of Sarmizegetusa from the west (forcing the Iron Gates), while the other assaulted them from the east. The Roman advance was very difficult and slow, the Dacian warriors putting up a fierce resistance and defending their homeland to the last man. The fortifications rebuilt by Decebalus after AD 102, however, proved to be of inferior quality compared to those that had been previously constructed with the assistance of Roman military engineers. As a result, they were all conquered by the advancing Romans and their garrisons were either destroyed or captured. By the end of the summer of AD 106, all the fortified Dacian positions around Sarmizegetusa had been taken and the two invading Roman columns could join forces. Trajan was now ready to besiege the Dacian capital, but he had to act very rapidly. He knew that winter was coming and it would have been impossible for his soldiers to conduct a long siege on high ground in freezing temperatures. The emperor, however, was determined not to make the same mistake again: Sarmizegetusa had to be taken and Decebalus had to be neutralized, at all costs. The siege of the Dacian capital, against all predictions, did not last long: the fighting was brutal, but the Dacians had lost most of their best warriors during previous combats and their population was exhausted. When the Roman soldiers entered the city, understanding that all was lost, many Dacian leaders committed suicide in order to avoid capture. Decebalus, however, did not consider the fall of his capital to be a mortal blow: he abandoned Sarmizegetusa before the end of the siege and moved north.

The Dacian king knew his realm very well and had a clear idea about how he could continue his resistance against the invaders. He therefore moved to the densely forested areas of the Carpathians, where he raised new forces and started planning another campaign to be conducted with guerrilla tactics because the Romans were now too numerous to be faced in a pitched battle. The northern portion of Dacia was the wildest of Decebalus' kingdom, being located far from the Danube and having no proper roads. Potentially, the Dacians could resist for years in the Carpathians; Decebalus, in fact, hoped that a lengthy resistance would buy him time to form new alliances with the Sarmatians and raise more warriors. Trajan, however, after conquering Sarmizegetusa, formed a special column of elite Roman troops and sent it to the north with orders to capture or kill Decebalus. The Dacian king was no longer a menace to the stability of the Empire, since he by then commanded only a few retainers. If not neutralized, however, he could have reassumed control over his kingdom in the future by organizing a revolt of the Dacians against the Romans. The

Detail of a Roman legionary attacking with the point of his *gladius* short sword. (*Photo and copyright by Legio XI C.P.F. Hispaniensis*)

troops sent to northern Dacia had great difficulties in finding their enemy and had to advance very slowly, as the terrain was perfect for ambushes and they had no idea of its extent. The Dacians obtained some minor successes in this phase of the war, usually by attacking small Roman parties with hit-and-run tactics. Time was running, however, and Decebalus had not yet been able to conclude a new alliance with the Sarmatians. His military resources remained limited and the Romans were gradually conquering northern Dacia. Eventually, during one of the many skirmishes that took place in this final phase of the conflict, Decebalus and his retainers were trapped by a Roman cavalry unit made up of auxiliaries. Surrounded by enemy soldiers, the great Dacian king committed suicide in order to avoid capture. All the other leaders who were with him did the same, leaving the Romans able to take only a handful of prisoners. The head of Decebalus was taken to Trajan a few days later.

With the death of the Dacian king, the war finally came to an end, although the Romans continued to fight for several more months in Dacia, putting down minor local revolts. By the end of AD 106, the former Dacian Kingdom had already been transformed into a Roman province, and the Empire now comprised a large portion of territory located north of the Danube. The fall of the Dacian Kingdom, however, did not mark the end of the Dacians as an independent people. Many of them abandoned their homeland after the Roman conquest and moved north in search of new lands where they could live according to their traditions. These soon became known as the Free Dacians, to distinguish them from the majority of the Dacians who remained in their homeland under Roman rule. The Free Dacians settled on territories that were already inhabited by peoples of Dacian stock and where the presence of the Sarmatians was quite significant. These areas are today part of south-western Ukraine, Moldavia and Bessarabia (a region of Romania). The two main communities of Dacian stock that already lived there were the Costoboci and the Carpi. The former lived between the Carpathians and the River Dniestr, while the latter inhabited an area between the Siret and Prut rivers. From an ethnic point of view they were Dacians, but they had never been included in the Dacian Kingdom. Over the decades they had been strongly influenced by the material culture of the Sarmatians and thus were quite different from the ordinary Dacians. The Costoboci and Carpi soon absorbed the refugees from the Dacian Kingdom inside their own communities, and thus became part of the Free Dacians. They then started to launch frequent raids against Roman Dacia, never accepting the loss of their homeland and always hoping that the Romans would abandon it. There was actually some basis to their hope, in that the northern borders of Dacia were particularly difficult to defend for the Romans: there was no great river like the Danube to use as a natural barrier and the frontier was too long to be defended with the construction of a wall.

Standard legionary *gladius*. (*Photo and copyright by Legio XIIII Gemina*)

Legionary *gladius* with plain bronze fittings on the scabbard. (*Photo by Marc Seriol [@marcmarkhus_photo] and copyright by Legio II Traiana Fortis – Cohors I Barcinonum, Barcino Oriens*)

Legionary *gladius* with decorated bronze fittings on the scabbard. (*Photo and copyright by Legio XIIII Gemina*)

Chapter 9

The Marcomannic Wars

Up to the outbreak of the Marcomannic Wars in AD 166, the military situation on the frontier between the Roman Empire and the Germani remained relatively quiet. Some Germanic tribes occasionally launched incursions across the Rhine, to which the Romans responded with punitive raids or brief campaigns; in general, however, very little changed from a political point of view, and thus the Romans could consolidate their *limes* on the Rhine. Only one event, taking place during AD 69 and 70, saw the Romans fighting on a large scale against the Germani: the Revolt of the Batavi. As we have seen, the Batavi had been conquered by the Romans several decades before and had been Rome's most loyal allies in Central Europe. They had participated in the campaign of Germanicus against Arminius and the invasion of Britain, and had even provided a chosen bodyguard to the emperors in Rome. In AD 69, Nero, who was particularly loved by the Batavi because he greatly appreciated their loyalty, committed suicide, after which the Roman Empire entered into a brief but bloody phase that was characterized by the outbreak of a civil war. In Roman history, AD 69 is known as the Year of the Four Emperors, since it saw the rapid rise and fall of three new rulers who tried to take the place of Nero. In the end, this internal struggle saw the ascendancy of Vespasian as emperor and the installation of a new dynasty, the Flavian one, which replaced the original Imperial family created by Augustus. The Year of the Four Emperors saw the disbandment of the *Germani corporis custodes* in Rome and a rapid change in the relationship that existed between the Romans and the Batavi. When Nero died, malcontent started to spread among the Batavi, who considered the disbanding of the *Germani corporis custodes* as an insult to their national pride. At that time the Batavi provided eight *cohortes* of infantry and one *ala* of cavalry to the Roman Army, which were attached to the XIV Legion. When Vitellius (one of the pretenders to Nero's throne) tried to raise more troops from the Batavi for his campaigns, the Germani rose up in open revolt and attacked the legion to which their units were attached.

Similarly to what happened in Germania with Arminius, the Batavian Revolt that took place in the modern Netherlands was guided by a hereditary prince who had served for a long time and with distinction in the Roman Army. This was Gaius Julius Civilis, who soon gained the upper hand in the campaign since most of the best Roman troops were fighting in the ongoing civil war. The Batavian leader was a man of experience, who had served as overall commander of the Batavian auxiliaries during the invasion of Britain. In the September of AD 69, the Batavi attacked the fortified camps of the two Roman legions that had been sent against them and obtained a brilliant victory, the two legions being forced to surrender after a long siege. The Romans were permitted to leave their camp according to the terms of a truce that was signed with Gaius Julius Civilis, but soon after having abandoned their positions they were ambushed by the Batavi. Both legions were destroyed and most of their commanders were enslaved. After this success, the Batavi were joined by several Gallic and Germanic tribes: the Batavian Revolt was expanding, but by now the Year of the Four Emperors was over and Vespasian had stabilized his control over the Empire. The new emperor assembled a large army of eight legions to crush the rebellion. The homeland of the Batavi was invaded by the Romans, who also had to fight against the Germani at sea since they had a strong fleet operating in the English Channel. The Batavi were eventually crushed and had to accept peace on humiliating terms: they lost any form of independence and their home territory started to be garrisoned on a permanent basis by the Roman Army. The events of the Batavian Revolt, albeit being the result of an ongoing Roman civil war, had shown once again the great military potential of the Germani. Indeed, a single Germanic tribe had been able to defeat two legions and to regain – albeit temporarily – its former autonomy. After the crushing of the revolt, the northern areas of the Empire remained largely peaceful for almost a century, until the outbreak of the Marcomannic Wars.

Also known as the *Bellum Germanicum et Sarmaticum*, the Marcomannic Wars were a series of conflicts that began in AD 166 and lasted for fourteen years, involving the clash between the Roman Army of Marcus Aurelius and the Germanic tribes of the Marcomanni and Quadi (supported by the Sarmatians, a nomadic people from the steppes of Central Asia). The struggle took place on the Danubian *limes* of the Roman Empire, along which the Marcomanni had lived since the days of Maroboduus. Around AD 160, in the vast plains of Eastern Europe, an important historical process known as the Great Migrations began. This happened, at least initially, far from the eyes of the Romans, but in the long run would have terrible consequences for the destiny of the Empire. Coming under pressure from the warlike steppe peoples who were migrating across Central Asia, the Germanic tribes living in Eastern Europe – such as the Goths – started to move west in search of peaceful new lands where they could live. The steppe peoples were nomadic communities with strong military traditions: thanks to their superior cavalry and the deadly use of the composite bow, they were able to easily defeat the eastern Germani and oblige them to abandon their homeland. In order to avoid destruction and retain their beloved

Officer *gladius* with decorated silver fittings on the scabbard. (*Photo and copyright by Legio XI C.P.F. Hispaniensis*)

freedom, the eastern Germani invaded the lands of the western Germani, who were forced to cross the borders of the Roman Empire in the hope of finding new lands where they could settle. Within a few years, the Romans started to feel an increasing pressure on their frontiers that was just the beginning of a much larger historical process which would finally cause the fall of the Empire.

Until AD 160, relations between the Marcomanni and the Romans had been quite amicable, with no significant conflicts having broken out along the western portion of the Danubian *limes*. The pressure applied by the movement of the Goths and other eastern tribes, however, changed this situation. Consequently, the Marcomanni tried to enter the borders of the Empire to establish themselves in Pannonia (present-day Hungary) and the other Roman provinces located south of the Danube. In AD 162, the Germanic tribes of the Chatti and of the Chauci moved against the western sector of the Danubian *limes*, only being repulsed after three years of incursions, then a group of Langobards invaded Pannonia for a short period in AD 166 before being crushed. These early incursions were the first signals of the beginning of the Great Migration, a process which the Romans had not yet understood. The Marcomanni, under their leader Ballomar, initially tried to mediate between the Romans and the other Germanic tribes, but at some point the eastern part of the Danubian border

Officer *gladius* with decorated silver fittings on the scabbard. (*Photo and copyright by Legio XIIII Gemina*)

also came under attack. Dacia, one of the largest and most recently conquered of the Roman provinces, was invested by the Vandals and the Sarmatians, who were able to obtain a decisive victory over the local garrisons.

The critical year of AD 166 also saw the emergence of another great problem for the Roman Empire. In that year, legionaries returning from a campaign against the Parthians in Mesopotamia brought with them – inside the borders of the Empire – a new disease that later became known as the Antonine Plague, from the name of the dynasty that was ruling Rome at the time. Within a few months the plague killed eight million Roman citizens and subjects and greatly weakened the Empire, at a moment that was already very critical for the stability of the Roman state. Marcus Aurelius reacted against the incursions of the Germanic tribes only in AD 168, when the plague ended: the economy of the Empire was in a perilous situation and the Roman Army was short of men. The emperor established his headquarters at Aquileia, in north-eastern Italy, and moved against the invaders of Pannonia. These tribesmen, who had initially been repulsed, had later been joined by the Marcomanni and returned to the Roman province during the difficult months that saw the spreading of the Antonine Plague. When Marcus Aurelius reached Pannonia with his forces, the Marcomanni crossed the Danube again to avoid a direct confrontation with the Romans. In AD 169, the emperor turned his attention to Dacia and fought against the Sarmatians, but obtained little success. At the same time, the Costoboci entered the Balkans from the north and raided as far south as Greece. The Marcomanni, sensing an opportunity, also crossed the Danube and invaded Pannonia again with a large number of warriors, having just formed a strong military alliance with the Quadi, another important Germanic tribe.

In AD 170, at the Battle of Carnutum, the Roman forces in Pannonia were utterly defeated by the Germani and suffered over 20,000 casualties. There are very few details about this clash, but what is known for sure is that it was a major setback for Marcus Aurelius. After obtaining such a great and unexpected victory, the Germani ravaged Noricum (modern Austria) and moved south towards Italy. The city of Aquileia was besieged, and for the first time in centuries the territory of the Italian peninsula was menaced by a foreign invader. By the end of AD 171, however, Marcus Aurelius had been able to mount an effective counter-offensive against the Germani, assembling all the military resources that were still available to him and relieving the besieged city of Aquileia. A few months later, the invaders were pushed back to the northern bank of the Danube. At this point the Quadi signed a temporary peace treaty with Rome, while the Marcomanni continued to fight. In AD 172, Marcus Aurelius crossed the great river and attacked Ballomar's homeland. The Roman offensive was successful and led to the defeat of the Marcomanni, but they still had

Legionary *gladius* with decorated bronze fittings on the scabbard. (*Photo by Marc Seriol [@marcmarkhus_photo] and copyright by Legio II Traiana Fortis – Cohors I Barcinonum, Barcino Oriens*)

Officer *gladius* with decorated silver fittings on the scabbard. (*Photo by Marc Seriol [@ arcmarkhus_photo] and copyright by Legio II Traiana Fortis – Cohors I Barcinonum, Barcino Oriens*)

significant military resources to deploy. In AD 173, the Quadi attacked the Romans again, breaking the peace treaty they had signed with the Empire. During that same year, the Germanic tribesmen of the Chatti and the Chauci launched several heavy raids against the Roman *limes* on the Rhine. Marcus Aurelius concentrated all his efforts against the Quadi, since he considered them, correctly, as the most dangerous menace to the stability of the Empire. In AD 174, the Germanic tribe was decisively defeated, after which the Quadi were forced to accept the presence of Roman garrisons on their territory, had to surrender all the prisoners and hostages who were in their hands and were obliged to provide auxiliary contingents to the Roman Army. Turning against the Sarmatians, the Romans then obtained some notable successes on the plains of Pannonia, and in AD 175 the Sarmatians also agreed to sign a peace treaty with Rome, according to which they were to contribute a total of 8,000 soldiers for service with the Empire. Some 5,500 of these warriors were sent to Britain, where they garrisoned the northern border and protected it from incursions by the Celtic raiders from Scotland. Before Marcus Aurelius could consolidate the Roman military presence north of the Danube, however, an internal revolt (headed by the usurper Gaius Avidius Cassius) broke out in the eastern provinces and prevented the emperor from expanding the Roman territories along the northern *limes*.

In AD 177, the Marcomanni and the Quadi revolted against the Romans and attacked the garrisons that were stationed on their territories. Although the Marcomanni were easily crushed by Marcus Aurelius, operations against the Quadi took longer to bring to a successful conclusion. Marcus Aurelius died in AD 180 while the campaign against the Germani was still going on, but the Romans had already prevailed in two pitched battles. Marcus Aurelius' son and successor, Commodus, had little interest in continuing the campaigns against the Germani and in stabilizing the northern frontiers of the Empire. As a result, he concluded a superficial peace treaty with the Marcomanni and the Quadi without solving the problems of the Danubian *limes*. After the end of the bloody Marcomannic Wars, which had tested the military resources of Rome to their limit, a total of sixteen legions started to be always stationed on the territories that bordered with the Germanic lands.

It is interesting to note that during the Marcomannic Wars, some of the first communities of Germani were permitted to settle inside the borders of the Roman Empire. Their members were known as *laeti* and consisted of defeated barbarians who received some lands in exchange for military service in the Roman Army. The Antonine Plague had depopulated large areas of the Empire, greatly reducing the recruiting potential of Rome, leading Marcus Aurelius to launch this early experiment. However, it was not a great success, as the defeated Germanic warriors soon rose up in revolt and even seized the important city of Ravenna (one of the Roman Navy's

Parade *gladius* with enamel plates and sculpted golden brass fittings on the scabbard. (*Photo by Marc Seriol [@ marcmarkhus_photo] and copyright by Legio II Traiana Fortis – Cohors I Barcinonum, Barcino Oriens*)

A display of five different types of *gladius* for officers. (*Photo and copyright by Legio XI C.P.F. Hispaniensis*)

main bases) for a brief period. The agreement granting land to a community of *laeti* might specify a once-and-for-all contribution of recruits or a fixed number of recruits required each year. The lands given to Germanic settlers were known as *terrae laeticae* and were not part of the normal provincial administration, since they were under the direct control of a specific administrative officer known as the *Praefectus Laetorum*. In addition to the Germani, a good number of Sarmatians were also settled in Italy and Gaul as military colonists.

Chapter 10

Roman Weapons and Tactics

When Augustus became princeps in 30 BC, the Roman Army already employed a highly standardized panoply which comprised some basic elements: helmet, armour, shield, heavy javelin, short sword and dagger. This had been introduced with the military reform of Gaius Marius, which was implemented shortly before the outbreak of the Roman Civil Wars. Under Augustus, the panoply of the Roman heavy infantrymen was altered in some of its components, but did not change in a radical way: new models of helmet were introduced, the previous *lorica hamata* armour was replaced with the new *lorica segmentata* and the original oval *scutum* shield was substituted by a new rectangular one. The tactics of the heavy infantry, however, remained more or less the same because the offensive weapons did not change. This new panoply continued to be used by the legionaries until the closing years of the second century AD, and was employed without modifications during the whole period taken into account in this book. The cavalrymen of the legions were equipped similarly to their foot companions, but continued to use *lorica hamata* and oval shields after the latter were ditched by the infantry. The offensive weapons of the horsemen consisted of a spear and long sword instead of the heavy javelin and short sword used by the legionaries. Until the military reforms of Augustus, the cavalry and light infantry of the auxiliaries did not have any standard equipment, with each group usually being equipped according to its own national fashion. With the development of the *auxilia* system, however, the many units of non-Roman auxiliaries that were created across the Empire also received a standardized set of equipment, which comprised the following elements: helmet, *lorica hamata* armour, oval shield, spear for the cavalry or light javelins for the infantry, and long sword for the mounted troops and short sword for those on foot.

At the beginning of the Imperial Period, the most common type of Roman *galea*, or helmet, was the Montefortino model. This was very easy to produce, the Romans having copied it from the Celts and introduced some minor adjustments that were needed to transform the Montefortino into the standard helmet of the legions. The name of this model of *galea* derives from the place in Italy where a first helmet of this kind was discovered. The Montefortino had a round shape with a raised central knob and a protruding neck guard; the former was usually surmounted by coloured plumes, while the latter was generally decorated with incisions. It also had a pair of cheek pieces, which could be of two different main kinds, according to their shape. The first model of cheek piece reproduced the stylized shape of the cheek, whereas the second one was trilobate, consisting of three small disks in the shape of a triangle. Apparently, trilobate cheek pieces were influenced by the helmets and armour of the Italic peoples, which frequently included this peculiar combination of three disks. Over time, this kind of cheek piece was abandoned and the other version became dominant, being the one adopted by the Romans. Montefortino helmets had many positive features: they were easy to produce, they gave excellent protection to the wearer's face, they could be easily decorated in many different ways and they were comfortable enough to be used for long periods of time. All these characteristics made the Montefortino the most popular helmet of the Roman Republican Period. During the early decades of the Empire, another helmet designed by the Celts and later adopted by the Romans co-existed with the Montefortino: the Coolus helmet. This had a simple round shape, with a ridge running around its base; at the back, this ridge enlarged to become a neck guard, similar to the one of the Montefortino. In addition, the Coolus helmet had a couple of cheek pieces that reproduced in a stylized way the human cheek. Being extremely easy and cheap to produce, the Coolus helmet became extremely popular, especially with the auxiliaries of the Roman Army. Archaeological finds suggest that cheek pieces were added to Coolus helmets only at a later date, as a result of the Montefortino's influence. As a result, at least initially, the Coolus helmet looked more or less like a simple metal cap. Crest fittings were only added at a later time.

From the last years of Augustus' long reign, both the Montefortino and the Coolus started to be replaced by what is known as the Imperial helmet. This was produced in two main sub-types – Imperial Gallic and Imperial Italic – which could in turn be divided into further sub-categories corresponding to different versions. The Imperial Gallic helmets, featuring a pair of distinctive embossed eyebrows on the forehead region and tending to be both carefully made and elaborately ornamented, were produced by the skilled Celtic craftsmen of Gaul, whereas the Imperial Italic helmets, lacking the eyebrows and being more roughly made, were produced by less-skilled 'copycats' working in Italy. Over time, however, the differences between these two main sub-types started to disappear since the Imperial Italic helmets also started to be of superior quality. Basically, the Imperial helmet was an improved version of the Montefortino one, having some more advanced features: sloped neck guard with ribbing at the nape, projecting ear guards, brass trim and decorative bosses. Following the combat experience gained during the Dacian campaigns, two iron bars riveted crosswise were added across the helmet skull in order to reinforce it, although as an

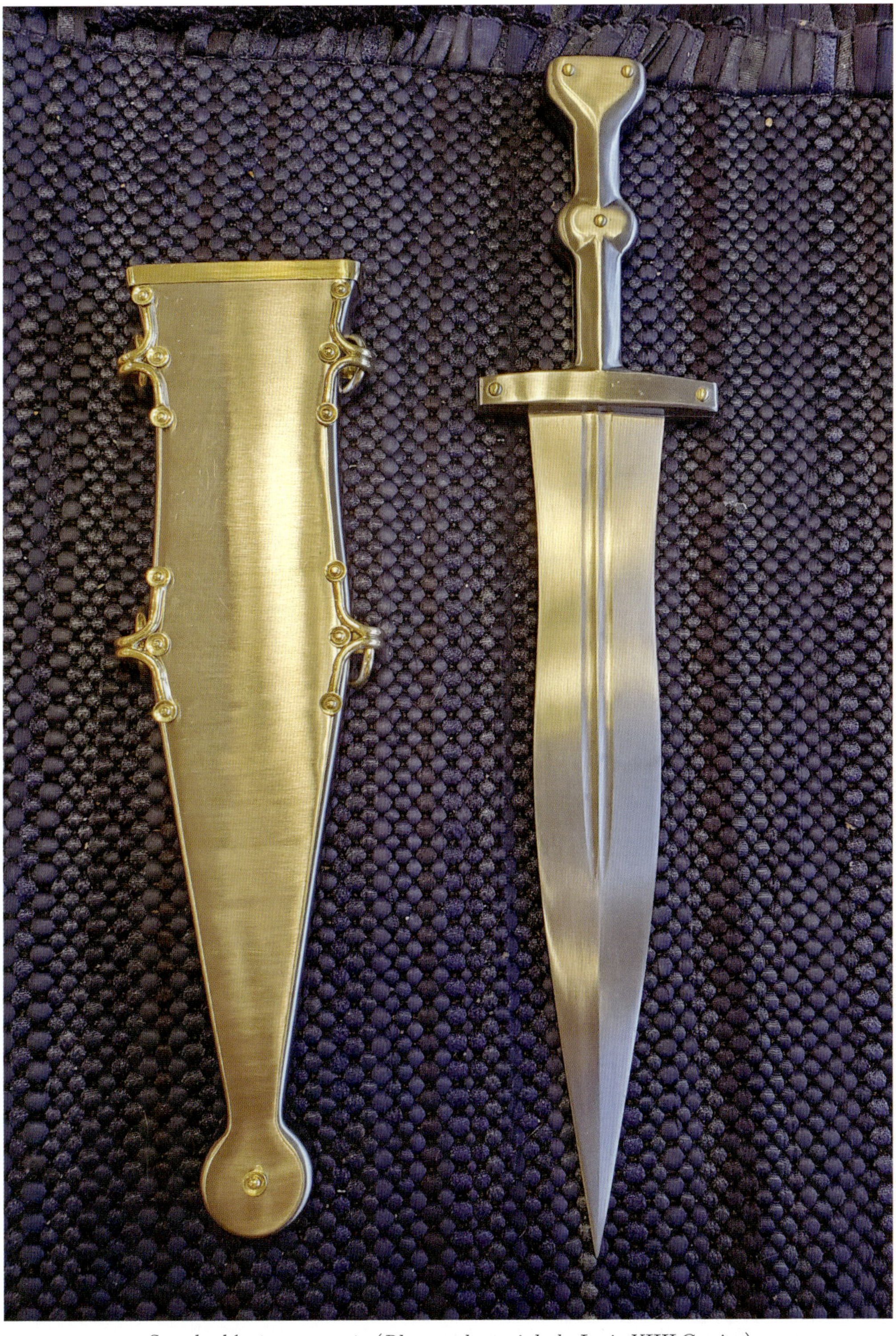

Standard legionary *pugio*. (*Photo and copyright by Legio XIIII Gemina*)

Legionary *pugio* with bronze scabbard. (*Photo and copyright by Legio XIIII Gemina*)

alternative, two thick bronze strips might be riveted to the top of the helmet. After AD 125, these modifications became permanent features. The Imperial Gallic helmet was produced in three main versions: the original 'G' version, the 'H' version that had a different style of eyebrows and a more sloping neck guard, and the later 'I' version that had a 'twist-on' crest holder instead of the previous 'slide-on' one. The latter version, differently from the previous two, was made of brass rather than of iron. The Imperial Italic helmet was produced in four main versions: the original 'D' and 'E' versions, which both had integral brass cross-braces placed flat against the skull but were decorated in different ways, the 'G' version that had brass decorations applied between the crossbars, and the 'H' version that was made of bronze instead of iron and had a deeper neck guard as well as embossed crossbars. This last version came into use around AD 180 and had a dome-shaped knob where the cross-braces met at the crown of the head.

The Roman *lorica hamata* was an improved version of the Celtic chainmail, which was designed for the first time during the fifth century BC. This consisted of thousands of small iron rings linked together in order to form a mesh: the rings were strongly interlocked, creating something similar to a knitted sweater. Depending on its dimensions, a chainmail was made up of some 30,000 metal rings and had an approximate weight of 10kg. Generally, Roman chainmail was sleeveless but had reinforcement panels for the shoulders, attached across the top of the back and held at the front by a bar-and-stud device. A double thong was stretched from the rings attached just above the inner corners of cut-outs to the outer corner of each of the reinforcement panels. The edges of the latter were bound with rawhide, in order to create a raised border. The panels could have angled or rounded-off ends on the chest, and they could be made of iron rings like the rest of the armour or could be of leather. The Roman *lorica hamata* comprised alternating rows of closed washer-like rings punched from iron sheets and rows of riveted rings made from drawn wire that ran horizontally, which produced very flexible, reliable and strong armour. Each ring had an inside diameter of about 5mm and an outside diameter of about 7mm. The estimated production time of an individual *lorica hamata* was two months, even with continual slave labour at the state-run factories. Although labour-intensive to manufacture, this kind of armour, with good maintenance, could be used by a soldier for several decades. Constant friction kept the rings of the *lorica hamata* free of rust, unlike the *lorica segmentata* which needed constant maintenance to prevent corrosion. The *lorica hamata* usually covered the legs as far as the knees. Until AD 10–15, all Roman soldiers wore chainmail armour, but thereafter the legionaries replaced it with the new *lorica segmentata*, and thus the *lorica hamata* continued to be worn only by the cavalry and the newly organized *auxilia* (both light infantry and cavalry).

The *lorica segmentata*, also known as the segmented cuirass, was without doubt the most advanced type of armour produced in the Mediterranean world during Antiquity. Thanks to archaeological finds, we know that the Roman legionaries fighting at the Battle of Teutoburg (AD 9) wore both *lorica hamata* and *lorica segmentata*, so it is possible to say that segmented armour became commonly used during the closing years of Augustus' reign. It consisted of overlapping metal strips or plates fashioned into circular bands, which were riveted to internal leather straps. The plates were made of soft iron on the inside and of rolled mild steel on the outside, in order to be hardened against damage but without becoming brittle. They were hardened by packing organic matter tightly around them and by heating them in a forge, in order to transfer carbon from the burnt materials into the surface of the metal. The plates were obtained from beating out ingots. The strips of each cuirass were arranged horizontally on the body, overlapping downwards; they surrounded the torso in two halves, being fastened at the front and at the back. The upper body and the shoulders were protected by additional metal strips. Thanks to its form, a *lorica segmentata* could be stored very compactly. It was possible to separate it into four sections, each

Legionary *pugio* and *cingulum militiae*. (*Photo by Marc Seriol* [*@marcmarkhus_photo*] *and copyright by Legio II Traiana Fortis – Cohors I Barcinonum, Barcino Oriens*)

of which would collapse on itself, thus forming a compact mass. The fitments that closed the various plate sections together could be of many different kinds (buckles, lobate hinges, hinged straps, tie-hooks and tie-rings), but were all made of brass. Over time, these started to be replaced by simple rivets. In addition, the lowest plates

Two different models of *pugio* and *cingulum militiae*; the one with plain scabbard was used by legionaries, while the other with decorated scabbard was used by officers. (*Photo and copyright by Legio XIIII Gemina*)

of the cuirass were replaced by a single and broader plate. Since all the components of the *lorica segmentata* moved in synchronization, this kind of armour was extremely flexible. It did, however, have two points of weakness: first, a legionary needed the help of a comrade to wear it; and second, it could be severely damaged by rust and thus always had to be kept clean. During the Dacian campaigns, in order to protect their arms and legs from the *falx* (sickle) used by most of Decebalus' warriors, the Roman legionaries started to wear some additional protective elements with their *lorica segmentata*. For protection of the arms they used the *manicae*, arm-guards made up of curved and overlapping metal plates that were fastened to leather straps. For protecting of the legs, meanwhile, they used simple metal greaves. A single *manica* consisted of one shoulder plate, about thirty-five strips made of iron or bronze, between ninety and 120 leathering rivets, three or four strips of leather and one padded lining. The metal strips were longer at the top of the arm and all had holes at their lower edge, through which rivets passed from the inside to hold the straps in place. The lower plates of a *manica*, overlapping upwards like all the others, could sometimes be riveted together in order to be stronger.

In addition to the *lorica hamata* and *lorica segmentata*, the Roman Army also used another two models of armour: the *lorica squamata* or scale armour, that was extremely popular in the eastern regions of the Empire, and the muscle cuirass, that was worn by the Praetorian Guard and officers. The *lorica squamata* was made from small metal scales sewn to a fabric backing. The individual scales (*squamae*) could be of iron or bronze, and the metal was generally not very thick, between 0.5mm and 0.8mm being a common range. Since the scales overlapped in every direction, however, the multiple layers gave good protection. Scales could have rounded, pointed or flat bottoms with the corners clipped off at an angle. They could be flat, slightly domed or have a raised midrib/edge. The scales were wired or laced together in horizontal rows that were then laced or sewn to the backing. Therefore, each scale had from four to twelve holes: two or more at each side for wiring to the next scale in the row, one or two at the top for fastening to the backing and sometimes one or two at the bottom to secure the scales to the backing or to each other. Sometimes, the *squamae* could be tinned. Scale armour was used by the legionaries, but also by the auxiliaries from the eastern provinces, including light infantrymen and archers. The muscle cuirass was a type of body armour cast to fit the wearer's torso and designed to mimic an idealized human body. It was cast in two pieces, the front and the back, which were later hammered together. The cuirasses of officers were highly ornamented with sculpted mythological scenes or with similar rich decorations. The muscle cuirass was used in combination with fringed strips of leather known as pteruges, which were worn at the armholes and at the lower edge of the cuirass.

Until the adoption of the *lorica segmentata*, the Roman legionaries used oval shields, which were copied from Celtic versions. These continued to be used by the cavalry and the auxiliaries after the legions adopted the new rectangular shields during the later years of Augustus' reign. The oblong Roman oval shield, or *scutum*, originally had a central spine made of wood and a boss (umbo) made of metal, which were designed to reinforce the whole structure of the shield. Bosses were oblong and could have different shapes. The main body of the shield was made of oak planks, which were chamfered to a thinner section towards the rim; the wooden spine, swelling in the middle, was shaped in order to correspond with a round or oval cut-out in the shield's centre. The strap-type metal boss crossed over the wider section of the spine and was riveted on the external surface of the shield. The surface, on both sides or only on the frontal one, was entirely covered with leather that could be painted in various bright colours and have decorations of several kinds. Bosses corresponded to the handle of the shield on the back and thus had a fundamental function in protecting the user's hand. Additional metal binding was frequently attached to the external edges of the shield in order to reinforce it. The oval shields carried by the

Pugio with decorated scabbard of the type used by officers. (*Photo and copyright by Legio XIIII Gemina*)

Detail of the *pilum* and the *sarcina* (the marching pack of the legionaries). (*Photo and copyright by Legio XIIII Gemina*)

light infantry and cavalry were generally a bit smaller than the heavy infantry ones and had a more circular shape; those used by the horsemen, in many cases, could also be hexagonal in shape and not oval. The rectangular *scutum* that replaced the previous oval shield was made from three sheets of wood glued together and covered with canvas, while over the canvas there was an external surface made of leather. The rectangular shield was convex and had a spindle-shaped boss along its vertical length. With an average weight of 6kg, it was 105.5cm high, 41cm wide and 30cm deep due to its semi-cylindrical nature. The mass production of the *scutum* was quite a complex procedure, considering the various phases that were needed to create a shield of good quality, but the shield's features gave a great tactical advantage to the legionary over his opponents. The rectangular shield was light enough to be held in one hand and was long enough to cover the entire wielder (making the soldier very unlikely to be hit by missile weapons). In addition, the metal umbo in the centre of the shield made it a punching weapon that could be used during hand-to-hand fighting. During the Dacian campaigns, metal edges were added to all Roman shield, since the *falx* wielded by Decebalus' warriors could easily penetrate and rip through a *scutum*. Most of the Roman shields were painted red and were decorated with highly standardized devices including eagles' wings, Jupiter's lightning bolts and laurel wreaths.

The first weapon to be used by a Roman legionary in battle was the *pilum*, a heavy javelin specifically designed to kill enemies from distance or to limit them in the use of their shields. The *pilum* was extremely difficult to remove after hitting a shield or a cuirass. It had a barbed head and a long, narrow socket or shank made of iron mounted on a wooden haft. The barbs were designed to lodge in the enemy shields so that the whole javelin could not be removed, while the long iron shank prevented the head from being cut from the shaft. The total weight of a *pilum* was between 1kg and 2kg, which gave the weapon great power of penetration. The shank, due to its peculiar function, was made of softer iron than the hard pyramidal tip; after hitting an enemy shield, it was designed to bend in order to render the weapon useless. The shank of the *pilum* was joined to the wooden shaft by either a socket or a flat tang, which was designed to break when the javelin hit its objective. Consequently, when a clash was over, the Roman soldiers could regain the wooden shafts from the battlefield and reuse them. The *pilum*, in most cases, had a spike on the end of the shaft that made it easier to dig into the ground. In addition, the javelin could sometimes be weighted by a lead ball in order to increase its power of penetration. The maximum range of a *pilum* was approximately 35 metres, although the effective range was 15–20 metres. The cavalry and light infantry of the *auxilia* were not equipped with the *pilum*, but with a lighter javelin known as the *verutum*. The shaft of this was about 1.1 metres long, much shorter than that of the *pilum*. The tapering point of the *verutum* measured

Side view of the legionary *caliga* military sandal. (*Photo by Marc Seriol* [*@marcmarkhus_photo*] *and copyright by Legio II Traiana Fortis – Cohors I Barcinonum, Barcino Oriens*)

about 13cm and had inferior armour-piercing capabilities compared with that of the heavier *pilum*. The *verutum* had a very simple design, since it lacked both the shank and the tang that could be found on the *pilum*. Both the legionary cavalry and several mounted units of *auxilia* were equipped with a thrusting spear known as the *hasta*, which had an iron point with an elongated shape – with the edges curving inwards from the belly of the blade to its tip – and a wooden shaft. The average length of this weapon was 2 metres, including a butt spike made of iron.

The *gladius* short sword, the most iconic and important weapon of the Roman Army, was actually not Roman at all. The true origins of this weapon are much clearer if we call it by its complete and proper name, the one used by the same Romans: *gladius Hispaniensis*. The *gladius* was first designed in Iberia, in the territories of modern Spain and Portugal, as confirmed by various Roman sources but also by archaeological evidence. It was created by the Celtiberians, one of the many warrior peoples inhabiting Iberia during the Iron Age. Differently from the other Iberians communities, the Celtiberians were of mixed descent, being the product of Celtic migrations across the Iberian peninsula. Because of their Celtic

The hobnailed sole of the legionary *caliga* military sandal. (*Photo by Marc Seriol [@marcmarkhus_photo] and copyright by Legio II Traiana Fortis – Cohors I Barcinonum, Barcino Oriens*)

heritage, the Celtiberians constructed weapons with very innovative techniques. The Romans abandoned their traditional Greek-style swords after the Second Punic War, as a result of their many encounters on the battlefield with the Celtiberian allies and mercenaries of Hannibal. They decided to adopt the same short swords as their Celtiberian opponents soon after recognizing that the *gladius* had great tactical potential. According to the latest metallurgical studies conducted on surviving Roman short swords, the *gladius* could be forged using two different kinds of manufacture: it could be produced from a single piece of steel or as a composite blade. Swords produced with the first process were created from a single bloom by forging from a temperature of 1237°C. The carbon content increased from 0.05–0.08 per cent on the back of the sword to 0.35–0.40 per cent on the blade, from which we can deduce that some form of carburization may have been used. Swords produced with the second process were crafted by the pattern welding process from five blooms reduced at a temperature of 1163°C. Five strips of varying carbon content were created: the central core of the sword contained the highest concentration of carbon (0.15–0.25 per cent); on its edges were placed four strips of low-carbon steel (with a concentration of 0.05–0.07 per cent) and the whole thing was welded together by forging on the pattern of hammer blows. Each blow increased the temperature enough to create a friction weld at that spot. The forging operation, the most important of the whole process, continued until the steel was cold, producing some central annealing. When produced by welding different strips together, the *gladius* had a channel down the centre of the blade; when produced by fashioning a single piece of steel, the blade had a rhomboidal cross-section. The blade of the *gladius* was two-edged for cutting and had a tapered point for stabbing during thrusting. A solid grip on the weapon was provided by a knobbed wooden hilt added to the blade, usually having ridges for the fingers. The hilt, known as the *capulus*, could be decorated in many different ways; the swords of high officers and Praetorians, for example, usually had a hilt sculpted to resemble the head of an eagle. Sometimes the blade could be ornate, for example with the owner's name engraved or punched.

The *gladius* continued to be produced during a very long time span, in several different designs. According to the traditional subdivision employed by military historians and archaeologists, the various types of *gladius* can be grouped into three main models: Mainz, Fulham and Pompeii (all named after the location where the prototype of each group was found). The original Iberian sword, used from around 200–20 BC, had a slight 'wasp-waist' or 'leaf-blade' curvature, which made it quite different from the following models. It was the largest and heaviest model of *gladius* ever produced, with a blade length of 60–68cm and a whole sword length of 75–85cm. The blade was 5cm wide, with the overall weight of the weapon being 900g. This

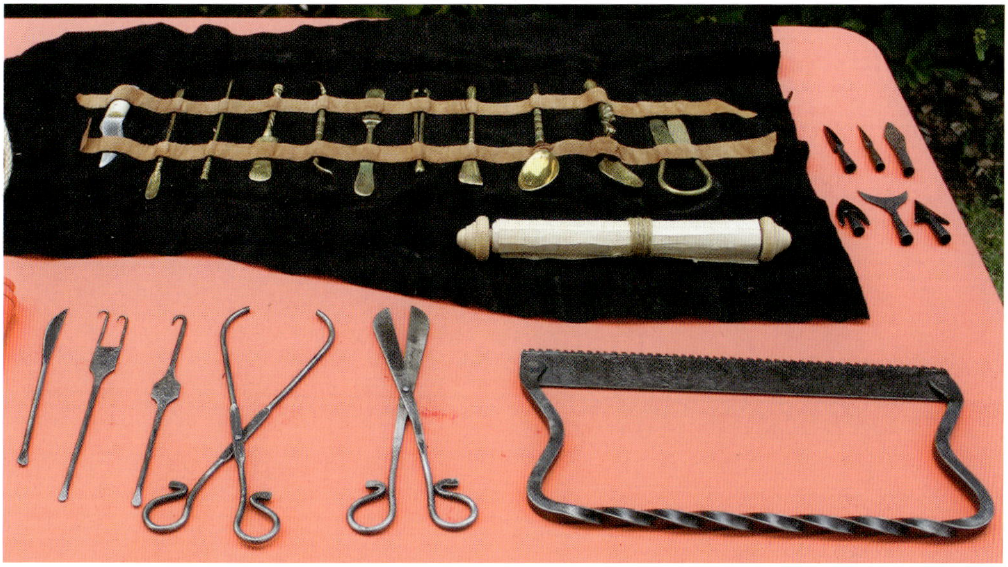

Roman surgery tools. (*Photo by Marc Seriol [@marcmarkhus_photo] and copyright by Legio II Traiana Fortis – Cohors I Barcinonum, Barcino Oriens*)

Display of the daily objects carried by a legionary in his sarcina. Note the presence of the *dolabra*, or military pickaxe. (*Photo and copyright by Legio XIIII Gemina*)

earliest form of short sword, still heavily influenced by the original Iberian design, was used for a very long period compared with its direct successors. The Roman city of Mainz was founded, like many other Roman cities, as a permanent military camp named Moguntiacum around 13 BC. The original military camp soon became

Roman *groma*, a surveying instrument employed by the legionaries to build their military camps. It consisted of a vertical staff with horizontal cross-pieces mounted at right angles on a bracket; each cross-piece had a plumb line hanging vertically at each end. This instrument was used to survey straight lines and right angles, thence squares or rectangles. (*Photo and copyright by Legio XIIII Gemina*)

an important centre for the production of swords and other military equipment, and with the transformation of the camp into a city, the manufacture of swords became even more significant, leading to the creation of a new kind of *gladius* commonly known as the Mainz *gladius*. The Mainz *gladius* kept the curvature of the previous model, but shortened and widened the blade. In addition, it modified the original point into a triangular one, specifically designed to thrust. The geographical diffusion of this model was limited to the border garrisons serving on the northern frontiers, differently from the less battle-effective Pompeii version that came into use in other areas of the Empire. The short swords produced at Mainz during the early Imperial period were employed by the legions serving in the north, along the *limes*, but not only there, as large numbers of these weapons were exported and sold extensively outside the boundaries of the Roman Empire. Apparently, various veteran ex-legionaries who had served on the frontier used their discharge bonus on retirement to set up in business as manufacturers and dealers of arms. The Mainz variety of the gladius was characterized by a slight waist running the length of the blade. The average Mainz *gladius* had a blade length of 50–55cm and a sword length of 65–70cm, while the blade was 7cm wide and the overall weight of the weapon was 800g.

The Fulham *gladius* derives its name from the fact that the original prototype of this model was dredged from the River Thames near Fulham. The Fulham *gladius* had a slightly narrower blade than the Mainz variety, but the main peculiarity of this model is its triangular tip. It had a blade length of 50–55cm and an overall length of 65–70cm. The blade was 6cm wide, and the overall weight of the weapon was 700g. The Pompeii *gladius* was undoubtedly the most popular of the three models that started to be produced after the original Iberian one, and had parallel cutting edges and a triangular tip. From a structural point of view, the Pompeii model eliminated the curvature, lengthened the blade and diminished the point. Regarding general dimensions, it was the shortest model of gladius: this was the result of battle experience from the Roman civil wars, during which Roman armies fought against each other in major pitched battles. In these cruel conflicts, because hand-to-hand tactics were employed by both sides the traditional Roman military superiority lost most of its efficiency. Fighting against enemies equipped exactly like themselves, with heavy cuirasses and shields, the Romans had to develop a lighter and shorter version of their sword, designed to thrust mainly with the point and in very strict spaces. The average Pompeii *gladius* had a blade length of 45–50cm and a sword length of 60–65cm. The blade was 5cm wide, and the weapon weighed 700g. Over the years, with the end of the Roman civil wars, the Pompeii *gladius* gradually became longer. All models of the *gladius* were carried in a scabbard mounted on a belt or, more frequently, on a shoulder strap. It was worn on the left side of the soldier's body,

View of a Roman military camp. (*Photo and copyright by Legio XIIII Gemina*)

so each legionary had to reach across his body to draw it. Centurions, to differentiate themselves from their common soldiers, wore the *gladius* on the right side of the body.

The Roman cavalry, be they legionary horsemen or auxiliaries, were not armed with the *gladius* of the foot legionaries and auxiliaries, but with a longer *spatha* cavalry sword. This weapon, originally designed by the Celts, had a distinctive elongated leaf shape, was double-edged and had a square-kink or shallow 'V' point (with the sides drawn at an angle of 45 degrees to the axis of the blade). The tang of the *spatha* – the internal part of the handle, made of metal but covered with organic material – swelled sharply to a point of greatest width that was just below its centre. The ricasso – the unsharpened length of blade just above the handle of the sword – was very short and had a notch that varied greatly in depth. Sword handles were made of wood or leather and generally had the form of an 'X', continuing the pattern of the famous Celtic 'antennae' swords. The handle was completed by a pommel, which was connected to the tang by a rivet-hole. The blade measured from 60–90cm in length and was made of iron or steel. Generally, blades had a broad neck, with the greatest width usually being low down towards the point. Over time, points became increasingly rounded, which confirms that these cavalry weapons were used for slashing and not for thrusting. Roman long swords were carried in iron scabbards, richly decorated with incisions and/or bosses. The scabbards reproduced the general shape of the blade and were constructed from two plates: the front one, slightly wider than the back one, was folded over the latter along the sides. Each scabbard was reinforced by a decorated band around the top and a sculpted chip at the bottom. Scabbards were generally suspended on the right hip from a belt made of leather, fixed to the waistbelt by means of a metal loop located at the back face of the scabbard.

Each Roman soldier, in addition to the *gladius* or *spatha*, also had a short dagger known as a *pugio*. This sidearm was intended as an auxiliary stabbing weapon, specifically designed for hand-to-hand combat. Like the *gladius* short sword, it was designed by the Celtiberians and later adopted by the Romans. The *pugio* had a quite large leaf-shaped blade, which usually narrowed from the shoulders to run parallel to about half of the length before narrowing to a sharp point. A midrib ran close to the length of each side, either standing out from the face or sunken by grooves on either side. The tang was wide and flat; the grip was riveted through it, as well as through the shoulders of the blade. The pommel was originally round, but it soon assumed a new trapezoidal shape. Each pugio was carried in its own sheath made of soft metal, which had four suspension rings and a bulbous terminal expansion that was pierced by a large rivet. The original design of the *pugio* was eventually slightly modified, with a rod tang introduced and the hilt no longer riveted through the tang since it started to be secured only at the shoulders of the blade. The hilt continued to consist of two layers of horn or wood. Each *pugio* was 18–28cm long and 5cm wide. The sheath could be heavily decorated, especially for the daggers used by officers or by members of the Praetorian Guard.

Each legionary carried a *sarcina*, or military pack, which comprised several important pieces of equipment. Since the days of Gaius Marius' military reforms, the Roman heavy infantrymen became famous because of their capabilities as combat engineers, being capable of building fortified camps or military infrastructures such as bridges in every condition and on every kind of terrain. The *sarcina* consisted of a *furca*, or carrying pole, to which the following objects were suspended: a *loculus* (leather satchel), a waterskin, a small bag with rations of food for fifteen days, a shallow *patera* dish, a cooking pot, a skewer, some pointed stakes (*sudis*) used to construct fortifications, a *dolabra* pickaxe, a *ligo* mattock, a *falx* used to clear overgrowth, a *batillum* shovel and a basket for hauling earth. The equipment of each legionary was completed by the *cingulum militiae*, or military belt, which had a very important symbolic significance: it denoted the wearer was part of the army, since civilians used different types of belt. Depriving a soldier of his military belt meant expelling him from the army. Basically, the *cingulum militiae* was a leather belt decorated with iron fittings and consisting of the following components: the *baltea*, or hanging band, the *bulla* (rivets that were applied on the *baltea*), the *pensilium* (pendants that were applied at the end of the belt's straps), the *lamna* (disk that was applied at the end of each apron strip forming the *pensilium*) and the *fibula*, or buckle of the belt.

In general terms, it is incorrect to speak of 'uniforms' for the armies of Antiquity, but we can say that the Roman Army of the early Empire had a high level of standardization in its dress, mainly due to the fact that state factories produced military clothing, equipment and weapons for all of Rome's soldiers. The main garment worn by the Roman soldier was the tunic: this was short-sleeved, but was also produced in a version with long sleeves known as the *tunica manicata*, which was commonly used in the northern provinces of the Empire. The Roman tunic, made of wool for cold months and linen for hot months, was a simple T-shaped garment reaching the knees of its wearer. It was not made of cut and sewn parts, but was woven entire in a single piece, with each *tunica* folded in half and sewn up the sides, a neck slit being cut in the centre. The standard colours for military tunics were red and white, the latter being extremely popular in the hottest regions of the eastern provinces. After the tunic, the cloak was the next most important garment worn by the Roman soldier. Made of wool and containing natural oil in order to repel water, it could be of two different kinds, known as the *sagum* and *paenula*. The *sagam*, typical of the Italic peninsula, was rectangular in shape, while the *paenula* was rounded and had a hood (*cuculia*) for protection of the head. All cloaks reached the hips and were double-folded so that they did not fall beneath the knees when worn. The cloaks of officers were quite different from those of the common soldiers, since they were longer (ankle-length) and trapezoidal in shape. All cloaks were pinned up on the right shoulder by a large brooch (*fibula*), which could be richly decorated if worn by a senior officer. The trousers, known as *bracae*, were considered by most well-educated Roman citizens to be a 'barbarian' garment, although the legions garrisoning the northern frontiers adopted them on a large scale from the early days of the Principate. All legionaries wore a *focale*, or scarf, around their neck; this was made of wool for winter and linen for summer. The *focale* protected the neck from chafing by the armour and was loosely knotted at the front. Regarding footwear, all Roman soldiers wore the famous open sandals known as *caligae* (whose name derived from the Emperor Caligula, who loved to wear them). They were made from leather and were laced up the centre of the foot as well as at the top of the ankle. Iron hobnails were hammered into their sole for added strength.

Roman legionaries deployed for an inspection. (*Photo by Marc Seriol [@marcmarkhus_photo] and copyright by Legio II Traiana Fortis – Cohors I Barcinonum, Barcino Oriens*)

Roman legionaries advancing on the battlefield in line. (*Photo and copyright by Legio XI C.P.F. Hispaniensis*)

Rank distinctions existed in the Roman Army. A centurion, for example, was distinguished as follows: he carried the *gladius* on the left side and the *pugio* on the right side (the legionaries did the opposite); he had a peculiar transverse crest on the helmet; he always carried a vine-stick (*vitis*) that was used to mete out punishments;

Roman legionaries throwing their javelins. (*Photo and copyright by David Burns of Legio XIIII Gemina*)

Roman legionaries advancing in *testudo* formation. (*Photo and copyright by David Burns of Legio XIIII Gemina*)

and he applied sculpted disks known as *phalerae* (made of gold, silver or bronze) on the front of his armour. The *phalerae* were military medals, usually awarded for distinguished conduct in action. They were aligned in three horizontal lines and were attached to orthogonal leather straps in order to form a single 'breastplate' that was worn on the chest. An *Optio* was easy to recognize since he had plumes of horse hair or feathers applied on either side of his helmet (with the standard crest in the middle), while he also carried a long wooden staff (*hastile*) that was as tall as the *Optio* himself and had a round metal pommel at its end. Like the vine-stick of centurions, this was used to mete out punishments. All standard-bearers carried a peculiar small round shield and wore a fur over their shoulders or head: a wolf fur was worn by the *Vexillifer*, a bear fur by the *Signifer* and a lion or tiger fur by the *Aquilifer*. The fur was worn as a cape, with the head of the animal strapped to the helmet of the standard-bearer. In many cases the standard-bearers, being veterans, wore on the chest the same *phalerae* as the centurions. The military musicians of a legion were usually equipped like the standard-bearers, carrying small round shields and wearing a fur over their shoulders or head.

Roman legionaries on the march. (*Photo and copyright by David Burns of Legio XIIII Gemina*)

Roman battle tactics were highly standardized but incredibly effective. The first weapon to be used in a pitched battle, as we have already seen, was the *pilum*, then once the enemy ranks had been shattered by the initial rain of javelins, the legionaries drew their short swords and charged their opponents. According to the Roman tactical doctrine, emphasis was put on using the *scutum* to provide maximum body coverage, while the *gladius* was used to attack with devastating thrusts and short cuts. Using these tactics, the Romans were able to defeat any enemy infantry for several centuries. This kind of warfare also limited the number of casualties suffered by the Imperial troops. Using their swords to thrust in the few spaces created between the shields of their close formations, the legionaries were rarely exposed to the offensive weapons of their enemies, who were given very little chance to manoeuvre. Like the *gladius*, the *pugio* dagger was a short stabbing weapon. It was used as a secondary arm during the most intense hand-to-hand fighting, especially when space for movement became very limited or when the *gladius* could not be used for any reason. Intensive and continuous training made the Roman legionaries highly efficient: the stabbing wounds produced by their short swords were almost always mortal, especially if hitting in the abdominal area (advocated as the main target for thrusts from the early phase of a legionary's intensive training). Each Roman infantryman was trained

Roman legionaries training with wooden short swords. (*Photo and copyright by Legio XI C.P.F. Hispaniensis*)

to adapt to any possible combat situation: each of his weapons could be used in different ways, and he had to be ready to exploit to the full any mistake of the enemy or any favourable momentum. For example, Roman legionaries were trained to slash kneecaps beneath their shield wall or to cut the throat of the enemies while charging in the famous *testudo* formation. In this turtle formation, the legionaries aligned their rectangular shields to form a packed oblong covered on all sides. The first row of men held their shields from about the height of their shins to their eyes, in order to present a shield wall to all sides. Those in the rear ranks placed their shields over their heads to protect the formation from above and balanced the shields on their helmets by overlapping them. The legionaries on the sides and rear of the *testudo* held their shields like those of the first row. The turtle formation of the Roman legions offered excellent all-round protection against the missile weapons of any possible opponent, and was inspirational in many victories for armies of the early Empire.

Bibliography

Primary sources

Appian, *Roman History.*
Appianus, *Gallic History.*
Appianus, *Illyrian Wars.*
Appianus, *Wars in Spain.*
Dio Cassiuss, *Roman History.*
Diodorus Siculus, *History.*
Diodorus Siculus, *Library of History.*
Dionysios of Halikarnassos, *Roman Antiquities.*
Livy, *History of Rome from its foundation.*
Plutarch, *Lives.*
Polybius, *The Histories.*
Strabo, *Geography.*
Tacitus, *The Histories.*
Tacitus, *Agricola.*
Tacitus, *The Annals.*

Secondary sources

Allen, S., *Celtic Warrior 300 BC–AD 100* (Osprey Publishing, 2001).
Anderson, E.B., *Cataphracts: Knights of the Ancient Eastern Empires* (Pen & Sword, 2016).
Baker, P., *Armies and Enemies of Imperial Rome* (Wargames Research Group, 1981).
Bishop, M.C. & Coulston, J.C., *Roman Military Equipment From the Punic Wars to the Fall of Rome (Oxbow Books, 2006).*
Brzezinski, R. & Mielczarek, M., *The Sarmatians 600 BC–AD 450* (Osprey Publishing, 2002).
Connolly, P., *Greece and Rome at War* (Frontline Books, 1981).
Cowan, R. & McBride, A., *Imperial Roman Legionary AD 161–284* (Osprey Publishing, 2003).
Cowan, R. & O'Brogain, S., *Roman Guardsman 62 BC–AD 324* (Osprey Publishing, 2014).
D'Amato, R., *Roman Centurions 753–31 BC* (Osprey Publishing, 2011).
Elliot, P., *Legions in Crisis: Transformation of the Roman Soldier AD 192–284* (Fonthill Media, 2014).
Goldsworthy, A., *The Fall of the West: The Slow Death of the Roman Superpower (*Weidenfeld & Nicolson, 2009).
Gorelik, K., *Warriors of Eurasia* (Montvert Publishing, 1995).
Kiley, K.F., *An illustrated Encyclopedia of the Uniforms of the Roman World* (Lorenz Books, 2012).
Macdowall, S. & McBride, A., *Germanic Warrior AD 236–568* (Osprey Publishing, 1996).
Matthews, K.D., *The Early Romans: Farmers to Empire Builders* (McGraw-Hill Books, 1973).
Newark, T., *Ancient Armies* (Concord Publications, 2000).

Newark, T., *Ancient Celts* (Concord Publications, 1997).
Newark, T., *Barbarians* (Concord Publications, 1998).
Newark, T., *Warlord Armies* (Concord Publications, 2004).
Nicolle, D. & McBride, A., *Rome's Enemies 5: the Desert Frontier* (Osprey Publishing, 1991).
Quesada Sanz, F., *Armas de Grecia y Roma* (La Esfera, 2014).
Rankow, B. & Hook, R., *The Praetorian Guard* (Osprey Publishing, 1994).
Rocca, S., *The Army of Herod the Great* (Osprey Publishing, 2009).
Rostaing, N., 'Lost Pontic legions: Pontic imitation legions used by Mithridates', *Ancient Warfare Magazine*, volume X, issue 3.
Simkins, M. & Embleton, R., *The Roman Army from Hadrian to Constantine* (Osprey Publishing, 1979).
Sumner, G., *Roman Military Clothing (1): 100 BC–AD 200* (Osprey Publishing, 2002)
Sumner, G., *Roman Military Clothing (2): AD 200–400* (Osprey Publishing, 2003).
Travis, J. & Travis, H., *Roman Body Armour* (Amberley, 2012).
Travis, J. & Travis, H., *Roman Helmets* (Amberley, 2015).
Travis, J. & Travis, H., *Roman Shields* (Amberley, 2014).
Warry, J., *Warfare in the Classical World* (Salamander Books, 1997).
Webber, C., *The Thracians 700 BC–AD 46* (Osprey Publishing, 2001).
Wilcox, P., *Rome's Enemies 1: Germanics and Dacians* (Osprey Publishing, 1982).
Wilcox, P., *Rome's Enemies 2: Gallic and British Celts* (Osprey Publishing, 1985).

The Re-enactors who Contributed to this Book

Ala I Batavorum

Some clouds of dust on the horizon, slowly heading in your direction… It turns out to be a squad of Roman cavalrymen, fully armed, each with shiny armour and a highly decorated horse. The approaching horsemen wear a silver mask, blinking in the sun, their faces covered, only showing their eyes: spectacular, yet terrifying. Stichting Ala I Batavorum recreates these cavalrymen from ages gone by. In our regular show, our fully equipped cavalrymen will show their skills at arms on horseback. Equipment and tactics will be shown and explained, both in single file as well as operating in a group. This way, all equipment and the tactical advantage of the cavalry within the Roman Army will be explained to the public. Entertainment at the max: a spectacular and educational show during your event that will have your guests talking about it for some time. Stichting Ala I Batavorum can bring together up to six cavalrymen. All our equipment is based upon the archaeological records and well researched. Our impressions focus mainly on the Batavian *auxilia* cavalry, but also include Augustinian and late Roman impressions. Most impressive is our late Roman *clibinarius* kit, incorporating a recreation of the Dura Europos (Syria) horse scale armour.

Contacts:
E-mail: info@ala-batavorum.nl
Website: www.ala-batavorum.nl
Facebook: https://m.facebook.com/ALA-BATAVORUM-133726753365976/

Legio II Traiana Fortis – Cohors I Barcinonum, Barcino Oriens

Barcino Oriens is a Roman historical re-enactment, reconstruction and disclosure group that was begun in 2009, at the Joan Pelegrí School in Barcelona, to spread the knowledge of ancient Roman history so that everyone can see, feel and touch it. 'Seeing' means presenting activities that bring us closer to the reality of the ancient Roman world. 'Feeling' means showing each historical reconstruction in the closest way to the interlocutor, so that he or she develops historical empathy. 'Touching' is making

Modern reconstruction of a Roman *ballista*. (*Photo and copyright by Legio XIIII Gemina*)

reality the objects, images, tools, costumes and various realities of Antiquity to bring them closer to the viewer. The purpose of the recreation and historical reconstruction of Barcino Oriens is, therefore, to link and let people know, in a direct, attractive and emotional way, our reality to that of our origins, to that of the Roman Barcino. With Legio II Traiana Fortis – Cohors I Barcinonum, we recreate and reconstruct differents aspects of a Roman legion. You can find out what the panoply was like, how the legionaries were recruited and trained, how they lived in a *contubernium*, what the battle orders and instructions were, and much more. Our historical reconstructions and re-enactments are always accompanied by a rigorous historical and academic explanation about each of the aspects shown in classical Roman Antiquity. We are educators of Roman history, spreading Catalonia's archaeological heritage. All our performances are theatrical stagings of different aspects of life in ancient Rome, from the daily life of the patrician ladies, through different aspects of military life: the way soldiers lived in a *contubernium*. It is a way of creating 'custom paintings' where these fragments of life are dramatized. All this is achieved through the performance of the members of the group, who create characters that are part of each painting and explain the situation following a script that makes them interact with each other and with the audience. Then, each of the performances becomes a small play (called a 'pill') that lasts between thirty and forty-five minutes (depending on each historical re-enactment), where the situation presented to the audience is dramatized. We want the crowd to understand and participate in it, immersing them in the atmosphere and the words of the characters, contemplating the material and costumes of our historical reconstruction. We want the audience to feel, live and touch the past through our representations, words and performances, and feel immersed in the world from 2,000 years ago. Ricard Llop Altés is the director of the group.

Contacts:
E-mail: barcinooriens@barcinooriens.cat
Website: www.barcinooriens.cat
Facebook: https://www.facebook.com/barcinooriens/

Legio XI C.P.F. Hispaniensis

Legio XI C.P.F. Hispaniensis was created on 7 July 2018, founded by veteran Spanish and Swiss re-enactors who wanted to build an accurate historical re-enactment group in Spain. Currently, the group has twenty-five members and rebuilds Cohort III of Legio XI during the first century AD (Flavian times). The group is twinned with the Legio XI groups of Switzerland, Belgium and Russia. It is considered the best-dressed group in Europe and has participated in events such as Augusta Raurica and Natale di Roma, in addition to training and military ceremonies, marches and camps. Several of its members recreate Roman horsemen. All the group's activities are characterized by a high level of accuracy and professionalism.

Contacts:
E-mail: cohorslemav@gmail.com
Facebook: https://www.facebook.com/LEGXICOHIII/

Roman *Optio* arming a *ballista*. (*Photo by Ricard Llop Altés taken at the re-enacting event Arelate 2018, copyright by Legio II Traiana Fortis – Cohors I Barcinonum, Barcino Oriens*)

Legio XIIII Gemina

Legio XIIII Gemina Martia Victrix is a re-enactment and living history group located in the United States, whose members are dedicated to representing the Roman legionary as he may have appeared during the years of the emperors from Nero to Trajan. We are a Roman re-enacting legion, with members from the United States and Canada; our group is based out of Ohio and surrounding states. We strive for authenticity with our impressions to better educate the general public. Founded in 2015, our group seeks to recreate the equipment, routines and experiences of Roman legionaries from the first century AD for public, private and educational events.

Contacts:
E-mail: info@legxiiii.com
Website: http://legxiiii.com/
Facebook: https://www.facebook.com/legioxiiii/?ref=page_internal

Lorica Romana

Lorica Romana (Legio X Gemina) is a historical reconstruction association that is implanted in the south of France near Nîmes (Nemausus). Our aim is to reproduce as faithfully as possible the 10th Legion of the Roman Army from the time of Caesar until the end of the second century AD. This initial approach has been extended to other related fields of Roman Antiquity. The presentation of civilian life, archers, Arecomic Volques auxiliaries and crafts thus allows us to get closer to other aspects of ancient civilization which left so many traces in our region. This approach is also accompanied by research in the context of archaeological experiments. This allows us to validate certain hypotheses and to stick as closely as possible to concrete reality. Apart from our services where the didactic approach and exchanges with the public are at the heart of our concerns, we also produce documentary films in order to promote the reviving of the heritage sites that constitute our common history. Combining fun and didactics, we fully participate to this desire to bring history to life. Daniel Pirosa is the group's president (Caivs Pirosvm Strabo) and Philippe Ciciarelli the vice-president (Decimvs Vorenvs Madavros).

Contacts:
E-mail: loricaromana@outlook.fr
Website: www.loricaromana.fr
Facebook: https://www.facebook.com/LoricaRomana/

Roman legionary using a *manuballista*, or 'hand *ballista*'. (*Photo and copyright by Legio XI C.P.F. Hispaniensis*)

Index